Hotel Dick

Hotel Dick

✦

Harlots, Starlets, Thieves & Sleaze

Steve Peacock

iUniverse, Inc.
New York Lincoln Shanghai

Hotel Dick
Harlots, Starlets, Thieves & Sleaze

iUniverse, Inc.

For information address:
iUniverse, Inc.
2021 Pine Lake Road, Suite 100
Lincoln, NE 68512
www.iuniverse.com

Hotel Dick in its entirety is a work of non-fiction. All incidents documented in this book have been witnessed by or relayed to the author. The anecdotes are guaranteed to be true and without exaggeration, although some names have been changed to protect the privacy of the innocent as well as the guilty. The author's experience as a plainclothes house officer, or hotel dick, as the position is traditionally known, is uniquely his own.
Everything contained within Hotel Dick took place from 1987–1992 at the Helmsley Palace, which as a business entity no longer exists. The state of affairs at the Palace as recounted in this manuscript is in no way intended to reflect the behavior of current guests or the management practices of its successor organization, The New York Palace. Contrasted to the lackadaisical safety and security record of the old Helmsley Palace attested to in these pages, it is the author's understanding—based on statements from several knowledgeable sources—that the New York Palace has instituted a professional and effective security program which greatly benefits its visitors and employees.

ISBN: 0-595-30464-8

Printed in the United States of America

To Jen

Poor man wanna be rich,

rich man wanna be king,

And a king ain't satisfied,

'til he rules everything.

Badlands, Bruce Springsteen

Contents

PART I
Money

Room Without a View

He's a *dead man*. Not quite deceased, but the old gent, crumpled before me on the floor of his luxury hotel suite, indeed is exiting this world quickly. Our mutual anxiety multiplies as his terrified tear-filled eyes meet mine.

I'm his last hope of surviving. We both know it.

"Operator, call 9-1-1," I shout into my portable radio. "Get an ambulance to room 1224. Elderly male. Possible stroke victim."

I lean on one knee next to him.

"What happened?"

No response. His face contorts, rippling under the strain of his futile attempt to speak. Lips quivering, cheeks reddening, he struggles to maintain eye contact.

"Can you speak?"

He shakes his head from side to side. Barely.

"But you can understand what I'm saying?"

He grunts, then quickly nods. His balding head twitches slightly. He whimpers, but that's it. He can't say what, at that moment, was registering in his head.

He clutches his leather wallet with the last remaining ounce of energy he could muster. The wad of greenbacks protruding from the wallet crunches in his pulsing grip. On again, off again. *Crunch. Crinkle.*

He's wearing only a t-shirt. That's as far as he's gotten. I guess that he must've taken a shower, dried off, and dropped to the floor soon after he puts the undershirt over his head.

The guest is an executive for a major high-tech company, which is holding its annual shareholders meeting that morning in the hotel's Versailles Ballroom. The agenda calls for him to deliver the opening remarks. A colleague of his phones security when he doesn't show up.

No doubt she's biting her fingernails at this point. But I decide she has to wait. True, the woman and her corporate counterparts have a more intimate concern for his well being. But it's *me* who's staring at him floundering on the floor, one foot in the grave. Saying, 'Excuse me, sir, I have to make a quick phone call,' just doesn't seem appropriate, even if it *is* on his behalf.

He's visibly uncomfortable that his genitals are exposed to a complete stranger—someone who very well may save his life (insofar as I call for an ambulance, that is). He tries to pull his legs up to cover his nakedness. It's not working.

I grab one of the plush terry cloth towels that's stacked on a shelf in the bathroom. Having covered his partially nude body, I sense that he's relieved.

"An ambulance is on the way," I remind him. "We'll take care of you."

He continues to grasp the wallet, his head and hands shaking slightly as he does so. He won't let go of the damn thing, as if worrying I'd take it from him. *You're wasting your energy*, I'm thinking. *I'm not going to snag your money.*

A gaudy hotel towel stretches horizontally—almost ornamentally—across him. The Helmsley Palace logo is perfectly legible on the towel. He's lying there with the logo screaming out the name of what the partially paralyzed man likely views as a tomb instead of a hotel.

I finally relieve him of one unnecessary burden, for him as well as for me.

"Sir, let me take that for you. I'll put it with the rest of your belongings."

He reluctantly releases the wallet. My eyes cris-cross the room to see if other valuables are around. More bills are stacked on an adjacent table. Several thousand dollars in large denominations. I scan the area further and see several other smaller piles of money around the room. *Am I overlooking something? Is foul play involved?*

I dismiss the idea. If someone caused harm to the old man, he or she would have robbed him of all his belongings, or at the very least all of his cash. That's just how the freaks and opportunists who occasionally filter through the Palace operate. Lose a $25,000 Rolex to a crook and you'll find that the perpetrator also walked out with your Louis Vuitton luggage set and the leather shoes from your feet.

But that's not the case here. My remaining unresolved concern is the existence of too much unsupervised money. Most of it's stacked on one table. Good reason to quickly secure the guest's belongings before the room filled with emergency responders.

It wouldn't have been the first time that personal property got swiped under such circumstances. As the first one—and initially the only one—on the scene, logically I'm the prime suspect if something disappears.

Fortunately, or so I thought, the security supervisor arrives. We immediately inventory the guest's valuables, which includes about five thousand bucks, a Rolex watch and a sterling-silver stapler from Tiffany's.

Slightly more cash is peeking from under a book on the dresser. I point this out to the boss. We hear the emergency crew rushing down the hallway. Before they arrive, my boss walks up to me and intentionally turns his back to the door behind him.

"Here. Put this in your pocket," he says.

He hands me the extra wad of bills that we had almost overlooked. I take it from him without saying a word. He waits for my next move, but I don't even blink. Then he says, "After all, this guy doesn't look like he's going to make it." A brief but awkward silence surrounds us before he walks away.

I then count what he had "given" me as he greets the paramedics at the door. It goes right in the envelope with the rest of the old man's belongings. Still can't figure out whether the boss was trying to hook me up or set me up.

The paramedics take the guest away on a stretcher. Once downstairs, they exit through the 50th Street side of the lobby, where the ambulance sits at the curb. I wonder if the guy is still worrying about his wallet and its contents. I deliver his possessions to the hotel cashier desk, where we lock them away in a safe deposit box.

I call an associate of the ailing guest, the same woman that first reported the soon-to-be-dead man's absence.

"I'm sorry. It doesn't look too good," I tell her. "They just took him to New York Hospital."

Returning to the security office, my boss immediately asks whether I had "taken care of, uh, that thing?"

"There was a total of $5,323," I say. "Including the $440 you handed me."

He purses his lips, shakes his head. Hands clasped, he leans back in the chair, squinting as if eyeing me for a clue. I walk away, disgusted.

This sense of disgust becomes magnified the following night, after the ailing guest's wife flies in from Georgia.

I come into work early to cover the tail end of the four-to-twelve shift, giving me the opportunity to call her to express my sympathies. It's sincere. And offering condolences is just one of those routine things that you do in a luxury hotel like the Palace. Although I'm a *hotel dick*, public relations is an unwritten element of my workload.

After identifying myself, I ask how everything is—meaning, of course, the status of her husband's condition. I explain I had found him after he was reported missing.

"Well, I am quite disappointed," she says.

I keep quiet. It sounds like she needs to vent. Okay. This is understandable, in light of her predicament. "I'm not pleased that a corner suite is not available."

Huh?

"And even worse is the fact that this room is facing the backside of a rather unattractive building. It's not something I expected from a hotel of this caliber," she complains. "And furthermore…"

I cut her off in mid-sentence, making no attempt to hide the fact that she's pissing me off in a big way.

"Ma'am, I really don't care how the view from your room is or isn't," I tell her. "I just wanted to know how your husband made out."

"Oh," she says abruptly. "Not well."

She doesn't elaborate, and I'm not about to press her for more info. I hang up before she could further bash me over the head with tales of her inconvenient travels.

I stare blankly at the wall. My partner, Robby, asks if I'm okay.

My voice cracks as I begin to speak.

"What did she say?" he asks.

"She's upset."

"No kidding. Her husband just had a stroke."

"That's not why she's upset," I say. "She doesn't like the view from her room. She bitched to me about the damn view from her room!"

I have to get out of the hotel, get some air. I figure a walk around the block will clear my head.

But once outside, my mind wanders. I stare at the towering spires of St. Patrick's Cathedral, just across the street on Madison Avenue. A trio of spotlights, perched upon the roof of the fifty-five story, one-thousand room Helmsley Palace, shine down upon St. Pat's. It's an awe-inspiring site, just slightly less spectacular than the view of the cathedral from around the twentieth floor of the Palace, just above the church spires, with Rockefeller Center serving as a backdrop.

The woman who had just complained about the view from her room would, instead, soon have a view of her spouse in a casket. And she'd be able to do it while playing with the damn wallet her husband had been so intent on keeping.

I wander the city, dazed, for about half an hour after the incident, muttering to myself, 'What the hell am I doing here? Why do I put up with this nonsense?"

Bronx Boy/Jersey Boy

These weren't difficult questions to answer. Simply put, I was a foreigner. Not of the immigrant variety, but an invited guest in a foreign land, of sorts. In fact, having been raised in the blue-collar world of the Bronx and later the Jersey Shore, I was at first honored to roam freely in such an environment. This was a world unlike anything my Irish ancestors or I had experienced.

Despite my humble beginnings just north of Manhattan, and later via the fifty-five-mile trip from Lakewood, New Jersey, to the Port Authority bus terminal on Forty-Second Street, I might as well have been a million miles away from the gaudy Italian-silk wallpaper and gold-leaf ceilings of 455 Madison Avenue.

As one of several plainclothes house security officers at the Helmsley Palace, I had five years to gaze at the underbelly of greed and gluttony, virtually unnoticed, like a fly on the wall. It was the side-by-side witnessing of ambition and success, arrogance and deception, human suffering amidst plenty. Few people get this chance to witness such extremes of…well, everything.

The Palace is a world of contradictions. Money and fame are in abundance. Equally so are signs of destitution, particularly on the midnight shift, when street people regularly walk into the lobby babbling—or simply escaping New York's frigid winter air. It's a life-or-death choice for some. And while some guests recoil in horror, others are quick to slip a twenty to a starving beggar or a quiet but plainly impoverished passerby.

The least expensive daily rate at the Palace at the time was about $250 for a single room. And that was just for a bed, three miniature chocolates on the night table and a maid to replace your stained sheets as needed. The further up the elevator you went, the larger and more expensive the suites become. The fourteenth floor was nice, but the forty-first floor was impressive—for twice the price. On the highest end were four three-level suites, each encompassing a corner of the fifty-third, fifty-fourth and fifty-fifth floors, replete with grand piano, cathedral ceiling and a personal elevator—all for only $2,500 a night, plus tax. Is it any wonder that only guests such as Elton John and Saudi Arabian royal family-members would stay in these luxury suites?

Actor Paul Hogan for three months lived in the posh Princess Grace triplex, named after the late Grace Kelly. Kelly stayed there shortly before her untimely and fatal car accident. Leona Helmsley, never one to miss a great marketing opportunity, named the suite in Kelly's honor or something like that. Right. I'm sure Leona was quite impressed with the princess, herself being the Princess of Brooklyn, after all.

Hogan's lengthy stay took place during the filming of *Crocodile Dundee II*, and it's likely the Australian star's Hollywood handlers picked up the multi-hundred-thousand dollar tab. Likewise, they made sure that Hogan had two hulking bodyguards waiting for him every morning in the lobby.

Never could figure out why they waited for Hogan downstairs rather than meet him at his room. Even the cheapest bodyguard is paid $25 per hour. You would think the studio would want its money's worth. Why bother protecting him only between the lobby and a limo parked outside the building? If anyone wanted to hurt him, they could've simply ambushed him as he exited the suite, long before his protectors would know something was wrong. Even when filming took place at night, specifically for the scene in Saks Fifth Avenue, his security staff waited in the lobby.

I guess they assumed hotel security would pick up the slack. Little did they know that at any given time at least half of house security was sleeping. I'll elaborate on that later.

Such babysitting of Hogan seemed unreasonable, as if it were simply for publicity's sake. Why the hell would anyone want to hurt the mild-mannered Hogan, anyhow? Then again, millions of people asked a similar question when Mark David Chapman murdered John Lennon a decade earlier, right on the other side of town.

The view from Hogan's triplex was breathtaking. The lower-level living room provided an unobstructed view of the Empire State Building and other New York landmarks through its twenty-foot windows. Whitney Houston had recorded the video to "I'm Your Baby Tonight" for that very reason, in that exact spot. The nighttime Manhattan background in the music video wasn't computer generated, as most people probably assumed. It was the real thing.

Gazing from the triplex's outdoor patio, taking in a 360-degree view of the city and the entire New York metropolitan area, was even more remarkable, even a bit dizzying. But casting my gaze upon the world-renowned New York skyline was a common occurrence. As a child, I had long admired the view from the window of our fourth-floor, pre-World War II apartment. We could see, in addition to the junkies in the park across the street, the George Washington Bridge on the immediate horizon and a million shimmering lights from Manhattan in the distance. After moving to the Jersey Shore, our frequent trips back to the city gave us a better although less frequent perspective of the grand skyline. Anyone who has ever ventured toward the Lincoln Tunnel, via the customary loop through Weehawken that takes you along and then under the Hudson River then on to Manhattan, knows exactly what I mean. The only view that tops it is—or should I say *was*—the view of the World Trade Center and the Wall Street area from across the East River in Brooklyn Heights. The devastation of Lower Manhattan aside, neither of these angles compared to the view from any of the triplexes of the Helmsley Palace.

Well, except maybe from a small landing just slightly above the rooftops, smack in the middle of the four luxury compartments.

Take Me to the Top

One New Year's Eve I decide to go up to that lonely rooftop, just before midnight. I punch in at 11:45, and immediately tell the rest of the security crew that I'm going on a floor patrol.

Although I regularly visit the triplexes when they're unoccupied, I ascend to the adjacent roof less often. It's only a small landing, a miniature roof-on-a-roof, if you will. It serves to house a blinding, pulsating red aviation-safety light. Not the most comforting place to be, especially in mid-winter with the wind whipping at your eyes and ears and a quarter mile of space is between your feet and the sidewalk.

I climb a wall-mounted ladder in the fire stairwell of the fifty-fifth floor. After opening the hatch, I look up at the illuminated, angular white roof of the eighty-plus story Citicorp building a few blocks away. The arches of the Fifty-Ninth Street Bridge, aglow in an array of lights, sit perched across the East River. A slow-moving barge and oil tanker pass one another as they headed toward the antique span from opposite directions. In the distance are the mainly lower-lying buildings of the borough of Queens, with so many thousands upon thousands of their flickering lights. Slightly south across the river is the historical but still-functioning Coca-Cola sign, its mammoth red letters brightly shining and reflecting off the water on the shores of Brooklyn. Facing downtown is the Empire State Building, its unmistakable spire draped in red, white and blue lights. Below Thirty Fourth Street the buildings typically drop down to a lower height, then rise again from Fourteenth to Wall, where the Twin Towers, at the time, stood majestically at the island's southernmost tip.

In addition to being bombarded by these visual stimuli is a corresponding audio feast. The faint yet consistent barrage of honking horns from below contributes to this multiplex of sights and sounds. A general hum comes from, without exaggeration, a million sources of noise floating upward from the streets of Manhattan, each indistinguishable yet collectively affecting what was spilling into my eardrums. Equally notable is the subdued roar of countless airplanes, all on their way to and from JFK, LaGuardia and Newark airports. One would never know that they're flying at many hundreds of miles an hour, as they seemed to drift like airborne snails adorned with steady, blinking lights.

I focus on a party that's taking place on the rooftop patio of the Princess Grace suite, about twenty yards away. As it gets closer to midnight, dozens of people are dancing and gradually winding down in anticipation of the first moment of the New Year. Suddenly, someone shuts off the music. All attention shifts to the living room inside the triplex, where the TV is on and the ball in Times Square, unseen to me, drops lower and lower. No need to look at my watch. The partygoers will soon explode with festive emotion, alerting me to the fact that both hands of the clock had reached twelve. A resounding cheer soon emerges from inside and outside the triplex. They turn up the music and resume dancing.

Don't Tell Me What I Need

I return to the lobby, watching an old woman at the edge of the hotel's grand staircase as she dramatically flips a white lace shawl over her shoulder. I watched from a distance as she repeats this task over and over. Couldn't tell if she's intentionally letting the shawl drop from her neck or if the item just wouldn't stay put. Either way, it serves to heighten a certain air about this decked-out senior, who continually looks about from left to right. A smile appears, fades, then reappears, as if every few moments another horde of adoring fans, unseen to anyone else, arrives to greet her. She's a sight, like an aging starlet that can't let go.

The Roaring Twenties ended, and someone forgot to tell her.

A gaudy headpiece adorns her skull, reminding me of something I had once seen in a low budget, early twentieth-century Hollywood epic. Wrapped around her head in a bun, a jewel-encrusted pin grasps the shiny material front and center, just above the forehead line. It looks like a miniature Nordic shield or a flattened Faberge egg is tacked to her dome to secure the silk wrapping. For all I know or care, it's an oversized Wal-Mart clearance item rather than an heirloom that should be stored in a vault.

Despite being dressed like an average guest in business attire, the current emptiness of the main foyer helps alert her to my presence. A nasty habit of standing as stiff as a secret service agent probably hastens her guess that I'm an employee. Having confirmed that I'm a lowly worker, she barks a request for a limo.

"The gentleman at the bell captain's desk can arrange that for you, ma'am," I say. I'm tolerant enough of her condescending tone to respond politely, but adequately irritated to send her away quickly. Or at least attempt to do so.

Her head slowly rolls from side to side, in steady intervals of about five seconds. She scans the lobby, visibly anxious, as if the last train out of town had already departed. I don't know if she's a nut-job in search of attention, or if she truly is on a mission to find someone in particular.

"Well I hope someone here can find a damn limo for me," she says. "What are you doing just standing there? Can't you call one for me?"

She quickly changes the subject, and her tone as well. "All I need is a limo to take my companion to the Waldorf." She abruptly walks toward the bellhop's desk. And then it hits me.

"Wait a second," I say. "The Waldorf is half a block away. You don't need a limo."

She pauses, eyebrows raised. Her face and head freeze, like the stunned look of the Frankenstein monster when he first arises from the operating table. Total shock.

"Don't tell me what I need!" she howls without blinking, having changed emotional direction once again. The hag takes a few awkward stutter steps toward me. "I know what I need and I need a limo now!"

There's no arguing with her. "The bell captain is right there, ma'am," I say. "He'll get you whatever you need."

Except for a stiff drink to calm down your grumpy self, I whisper.

In less than half an hour, a spiffy-looking man that likewise appears to have been born around the turn of the last century meets her in the lobby. A stretch limo pulls up and a doorman summons them.

I step outside and watched the limo cross Park Avenue. Within seconds it arrived at the Waldorf. Do you remember the movie *Coming to America* with Eddie Murphy? How about the scene in which Murphy, playing the role of an African prince in search of a bride in America, bolts from a cab and runs across the street in the pouring rain? I had watched the filming of that scene a few months earlier from a vacant room, on the Park Avenue side of the Palace. It took Murphy just a few seconds to cross the street.

The drive from the Palace to the Waldorf takes a couple of seconds more. Despite the four-hour minimum, seventy-five dollar per hour price tag, Lady Frankenstein gladly forks over three hundred bucks to be driven a few hundred feet.

Dreaming of Genies

Emerging from the Palace Tower elevators one morning is a steady stream of young women, all decked out like Jasmine from Disney's *Aladdin*, similar to the main character in the sixties sitcom *I Dream of Genie,* minus the cleavage. No less than two dozen such characters line up and faced one another, forming two rows in the main lobby, while several bodyguard-types in suits hover around the perimeter of the spectacle.

No one from management had advised me that such activity is to take place, but I'm not about to stop them and ask what the hell they're doing. It's pretty obvious that they all belong here. Dozens of Middle Easterners typically don't appear from the Towers, line up in the lobby like toy soldiers and turn out to be trespassers. I continue to watch, quietly.

Several other stone-faced men in suits come out of the Towers and enter the main lobby, where they escort a young lady to the genie ritual. The genies bow as she struts straight down the middle of the rows. The chief genie is kind to them, greeting each one she passes. The entourage then follows her up the main staircase to the mezzanine. Her personal security staff scours the area nervously as they lead her to the Versailles Ballroom.

One day earlier the ballroom was attended to by squads of technicians, ranging from stage hands to sound engineers. It took a full day to assemble a concert-size stage, accompanied by an elaborate lighting and sound system. The arrangement was immense and quite complex as far as ballrooms are concerned, as if prepared for the next leg of a Pearl Jam world tour.

Likewise, it had been staffed overnight by a private security force. No one was allowed to enter the ballroom, not even hotel security.

The focal point of this extravagance turns out to be the Princess of Brunei, daughter of the Sultan of Brunei, who at the time is the richest man on earth. Even richer than Microsoft's Bill Gates, who in the late eighties is still relatively small-time compared to the Sultan.

Although I know that the princess is staying at the hotel, I don't realize she's having what I assume is a banquet or some other gathering in the ballroom. I'm aware that *someone* has rented the ballroom for three days, but again have no clue why.

It turns out that it's for the princess's morning exercise routine. Yes, she's renting an entire ballroom, adorned with crystal lighting fixtures and antique paintings of plantation owners and their slaves, so she can prance around in private. The Versailles room is costing $25,000 a day to rent. And here's someone reserving it for three days.

To top it off, she puts it to good use for just one morning.

Seventy-five grand for the room, tens of thousands of dollars more for the equipment and thousands more for round-the-clock security to make sure no one plants a bomb in the princess's temporary playground. All of this just in case she feels compelled to exercise. Lump that in with a $1,000-a-night suite and an additional full floor of rooms to house dozens of traveling staff members and servants.

The Brunei royals must really like the Palace. A few years later, they buy it for an undisclosed sum and renamed it the New York Palace.

It's hard not to be fascinated by the sudden appearance of a princess. This isn't Snow White, after all. It's the real deal.

Can't say I'm not in awe of the spectacle. But to think of the resources being invested to accommodate every whim of this one person, it's difficult not to feel a wrenching knot in the stomach.

I have a similar reaction to the arrival of Jean Bertrand Aristide, then president of Haiti.

Haitian Divorce

A fleet of massive Chevy Suburbans with tinted windows descends on the Palace without warning. Despite the crush of midday traffic, government agents abruptly block Fiftieth Street. All vehicles, including cross-town buses, are steered north onto Madison Avenue, causing a massive traffic jam. But the snarling cars and buses are of no importance to the feds. Anyone who dares question the actions of these machine gun-toting robots will be dragged from their vehicles and arrested. In fact, despite identifying myself as a member of house security, they strongly encourage me to take a walk when they arrive at the hotel entrance. And I do.

An additional phalanx of Suburbans surrounds a black stretch limo that pulls up. Seeing that Uzis were sticking out every window, I back up further into the lobby. A small army of feds then sweep Aristide into the building and to an awaiting elevator.

No one can go near those elevators. It doesn't matter who you are—or who you *think* you are. They don't care if even Michael Jackson or Elton John want to get to their suites. The agents emanate a clear yet quiet message to stay away.

Aristide at the time had been overthrown in a military coup that a small but elite class of Haitians had instigated. I had watched much of this unfold on TV a day or two earlier. These Third World power brokers despised him for speaking on behalf of the poor, who until this day still comprise the vast majority of Haitians. Having risen from ghetto preacher to president, wealthy Haitian landowners saw Aristide as an immediate threat. He had dared to question why they controlled vast swaths of land in a nation where people on average earned the equivalent of $26 annually.

As far as I can tell, the exiled Aristide, once a populist of the people, is living in posh quarters that few of his supporters could have envisioned, I'm sure. He temporarily stays in the Palace Towers, adjacent to rock stars, princesses and oil sheiks, under the watchful eye of the U.S. State Department. Perhaps I'm being too judgmental. That same week he's scheduled to address the United Nations General Assembly, also on the East Side of Manhattan. For all I know, the U.S. government is insisting that he stay at the Palace as a matter of logistics until a semipermanent home is found for him. He isn't living under ideal circumstances, don't get me wrong. Some people want to see him dead. But he's living like a king nonetheless.

Burning the Benjamins

Harry's Bar, located on the Fifty-First Street side of the hotel lobby, is a magnet for guests and other visitors to the city to sit down and unwind. Whether they want to sip on the most expensive wine on earth and eat shrimp longer than a baby's arm, or if they just need to belt down a few beers and chow down on a twelve-dollar burger, some view it as the quintessential New York City bar.

Advertising executives come in and recruit a Harry's bartender for beer commercials. In fact, there's a Budweiser ad that was broadcast throughout the early nineties that began with a bartender filling a mug from a tap and then sliding it to former New York Mets slugger Rusty Staub. That bartender is John Duffy, who for more than decade served drinks and smiles to thousands of Palace visitors.

Although it appears to be a civil place, for some it's just another venue to brag, a stage to exclaim the apparent virtues of wealth.

Two such stellar capitalists seeking bragging rights sit next to each other one night at the bar. They're strangers. Both are in their late fifties, maybe early sixties, each dressed in jacket and tie. As the hours of drinking continue, however, their collar buttons become undone, their ties gradually loosen, the knots on their neck-pieces sloppily hang lower on their chests.

Their behavior *regressed* as the evening *progressed*, no less competitive than male peacocks screeching while displaying an array of brightly colored feathers to impress potential mates. It wasn't unusual to watch a guest walk into Harry's as a sophisticated looking gentleman, then exit hours later a different man, no less out-of-control than any Joe on a Friday night stumbling out of a working-class bar on Third Avenue.

As I recall, their conversation went more or less as follows:

"You should see the fleet of antique cars I own. I've got them under lock and key in a guarded warehouse, which I also own," elite drunk number-one says.

"So what," drunk number-two responds. "I've got a pool as big as the hotel lobby, and a bathhouse next to it that's probably bigger than the damn house you live in."

"My house?" he chuckles as he stands from his seat. "Which one?" He laughs loudly, coughing loose phlegm, as old drunks do.

The other arises abruptly, as if not to be intimidated by his opponent's last move. His wobbly stance reveals the state of affairs inside his cognac-soaked brain. He reaches into his pocket, retrieving a wallet and pulling out a hundred-dollar bill.

"I've got so much money, I can burn this C-note quicker than you'd throw a penny into a wishing well!" he shouts. He lights a match and sets the bill ablaze. After dropping it into an ashtray, he looks around smiling smugly, as if this feat can't be outdone.

His opponent, however, who pulls a thick wad of hundreds from a money clip, isn't impressed.

"I can burn ten bills for every one that you burn, mister!" He fumbles for a silver lighter in his pocket. With a *ka-ching* from his Zippo, a thousand dollars disappears before everyone's eyes.

While the response of Harry's other occupants ranges from mild annoyance to amusement, the bar's staff is mortified. Shouts of *You fools! and Leave your money as a tip if you want to get rid of it!* alternately come from behind the bar and across the room from the table servers.

A brief shoving match ensues between the two amateur arsonists before they're separated then escorted to opposite ends of the lobby.

The piano player resumes his act. The other guests return to their conversations, as if nothing happened.

The employees, most of whom are blue-collar folks from the outer boroughs and New Jersey, stare blankly at one another.

None was looking for a hand-out. It's just that they bust their butts every day to pay the bills and hopefully have enough left over at the end of the year to vacation with the kids. Their attitude understandably was along the lines of, 'If you're going to throw away money, then throw it this way.' In that regard, the busboy from El Salvador, the waitress from Romania, and the Irish- and African-American bartenders had a lot in common.

They stare for a moment at the ashtray full of smoldering bills.

"It would take me a week or more to make what they just burned," one of the bar-backs says. He stands looking at the smoky cinders, which silently swirl behind him like frankincense following a priest down the aisle in a Catholic funeral ceremony. He doesn't bother emptying the ashtray. Just slams it into the garbage can, as if purging the bar of all remnants of the bill-burning spectacle.

She's Breathing, Isn't She?

At the start of a rare day shift I had been working, my partner Ron and I responded to a room whose occupants had requested a doctor. The person who made the call hadn't told the service operator what was wrong, nor did they say they had an emergency. It wasn't until we arrived at the room that we realized the extent of the problem at hand.

The blip of light from the peephole suddenly darkens. Someone reacts to our knocking, but doesn't open the door. He or she is intentionally silent, apparently assuming we're oblivious to that individual's presence. We knock again, this time loudly.

"Who is it?" the still-hidden person asks nervously.

"It's house security, sir. Did you request a doctor?"

A man wearing a suit, maybe in his late thirties, early forties, opens the door, annoyed, and shouts, "I asked for a doctor, not a couple of security guards!"

"Fine," Ron responds. "Wait for a doctor then."

Ron throws his hands in the air and walks away. I later regret that I hadn't done the same. Ron, who's been in the hotel business much longer than me, has a low tolerance for baloney from the guests. Although his reaction is appropriate, I have a gut feeling to press the issue.

"Excuse me, sir, but we're trained in first aid. Maybe we can help if you just relax and tell us what's going on," I say.

He reluctantly lets us in, leading us past his wife and kids into an adjacent room. On the bed is an elderly female. She's breathing, but unconscious.

This isn't a situation in which you wait for your personal doctor to arrive. I tell the hotel operator to call 9-1-1 immediately.

Ron and I look at each other and shake our heads in disgust. Any normal human being would have called for an ambulance without hesitation. These seem to be otherwise intelligent people. It makes no sense to have made a simple "sick call." I confront them about it.

"Did you happen to notice that she isn't conscious?" I ask

After looking at his watch the guy replies, "Well, um, she's breathing, isn't she?"

His poorly timed sarcasm burns into my brain. This poor woman is motionless on the bed, barely breathing, and her heartless son-in-law gets snotty with me as if I had no right to question him. Grabbing the sarcastic bastard by the throat and slamming him against the wall is an appealing move at the time. Ron senses this, and simply lays a reassuring hand on my shoulder, bringing me back to my senses. I relent.

The ambulance arrives just as the woman's breathing becomes abruptly shallow. Ron and I step into the hallway as the emergency medical technicians try to revive her.

We overhear the guest telling his wife, "Honey, this is an important meeting I have to go to. I'll call you when I get to Cleveland."

He picks up his briefcase and walks out of the room. His gait is stiff, as if splints are restraining his arms and legs. It's impossible to tell whether his tension is the by-product of the situation or if he's agitated by the prospect of having to rush to the airport.

"Is he doing what I think he's doing?" Ron asks.

We stare in disbelief as he heads toward the elevators.

"Imagine that, Ron," I bellow, "leaving your wife and kids with your dying mother-in-law so you can take care of a business meeting."

I reluctantly continue, "What kind of loser would do such a thing?"

This stops him in his tracks. He turns around and heads back to the room, apologizing to his wife.

"Perhaps I should stay," he sheepishly admits.

Moments later the elderly woman lapses into cardiac arrest. She dies soon after. The EMTs exit the building with the corpse. Ron and I return to the lobby.

As the ambulance disappears across East Fiftieth Street, one of the doormen asks what happened. After hearing the woman had passed away he says, "I'm not surprised."

"Why do you say that?" I ask.

"She's nearly ninety years old. They fly her all the way across the country, drive her around Manhattan all weekend, then top it off by going dancing at the Palladium. It's no wonder they're carrying her out of here."

"It makes you wonder what the hell they were thinking," I add.

Later that day I spot the family of the deceased standing in the lobby, smiling and shaking hands with a couple of men, lawyers by the looks of the wide briefcases they carry. Only a few hours after the incident, they're laughing and smiling as if they had just won the lottery.

The adults seem at ease. The kids stand at their side, however, silent as stage props.

Where Eez My Wife?

An anonymous guest registers a noise complaint with the service operator, who dispatches me to the twenty-ninth floor with no further details. It's safe to assume it's another routine call involving a whining guest. A purportedly loud TV, an imaginary person lurking in the hallway, something like that. Get those complaints almost every night. No problem.

The elevator door opens when I get upstairs. In muffled intervals, I hear feet pounding the rug. It speeds up—gets closer, louder. Someone is running toward me, but the elevator bank is out of sight from most guestrooms and at first I see nothing. As if testing the temperature of swimming pool, I dip my right foot onto the hallway rug rather than lunge my body forward in its entirety, just in case the water isn't inviting. Despite the lack of a visual of the still-unseen figure, what begins as a nearly inaudible whimper has now erupted into a panic-stricken, ear-piercing howl. A near- collision with a woman who's aiming for the open doors of the elevator follows. She's covered with blood. The red stream flows from the top of her head, through matted strands of hair and semicircular paths of ear cartilage, and rests momentarily on her shoulders. No match for gravity, her life-liquid makes its way down her nightshirt, which is soaked down to the crotch. Some has dripped along her legs, in fact. I watch as she bounces off the four walls like a pinball, clutching at the gash in her head.

Keep in mind I have no idea at this point what has happened. In other words, there's a chance her attacker is hiding nearby. Although getting a towel from the housekeeper's closet down the hallway will enable me to put pressure on her wound, it's too risky. I'm taking the express shuttle to the lobby, for the sake of survival. Let NYPD search for the suspect.

Kissing the radio transmitter, I yell, "Operator, call 9-1-1! Get the cops and an ambulance to the twenty-ninth floor quickly. Guest with a massive head wound, bleeding badly."

The battery turns out to be dead. Luckily, the sicko that assaulted this woman isn't approaching

She alternately chokes and pants between howls of agony as we descend to the ground floor. I try to find out what happened, maybe get a description of the perpetrator. But she only sobs and stutters rapidly in Spanish. Can't understand a word she says.

Collapsing to the floor, she begins losing consciousness. We finally reach the lobby. I scream for help.

"Somebody get over here! Call the cops!"

The night manager runs right over to us. Unfortunately for her, she looks into the elevator before I could explain what little I knew about the situation, before giving her a warning about what she was about to see. She gasps, her face revealing horror as if opening a trunk containing a rotted corpse. Nearly faints, in fact.

"My radio's dead. Call 9-1-1 and please get some towels. She's got a crack in her skull."

This scene is bad enough for anyone to witness. But it's even worse for this particular manager to stumble across.

Shawanda, who recently transferred to the Palace from the Forty-Second Street Helmsley, had already made a gruesome discovery in her short career. In a previous encounter, she had stepped away from the front desk, annoyed that a set of elevator doors were repeatedly opening and closing for no plain reason.

A murdered house officer lay dead at her feet. Minutes earlier he had walked into a burglar who panicked and stabbed him in the heart before escaping. The employee lived long enough to make it to the elevator, then silently died as he tried to crawl out of the compartment and onto the main floor.

Having seen this second bloody mess, Shawanda resigned soon after. Became a postal worker, if I'm not mistaken. Seriously.

We wrap the ailing guest in a bathrobe and take her to a nearby manager's office. I try placing a towel on the gaping wound on her head, but she won't hold still. She's not only drunk, but understandably traumatized, a step away from unconsciousness. The paramedics and the cops arrive simultaneously, all of whom speak Spanish.

I should've known something bad was going to happen that night. During an earlier patrol of the lobby, I suddenly heard sounds coming from the check-in desk that reminded me of the garrulous noises made by Chewbacca, the hairy ape-like character from the Star Wars trilogy. It's troubling to hear and not simultaneously see the source of animal sounds at three in the morning. The two-legged creatures that typically walked into the hotel in the middle of the night were scary at times, but always were distinctly humanoid.

I tiptoe toward the Fiftieth Street side of the lobby where the animal sounds originate. I gradually poke my head around the corner of the cashier's desk, letting my imagination imagine sharp claws dripping with blood turning the corner simultaneously.

But there are no wolves in sight. And no rats the size of Leona Helmsley. Just a drunk, middle-aged couple who arrived in New York from Mexico City, arguing in Spanish and alternately wobbling into each other and falling to the floor. It's a mess.

A bellhop slowly rolls a luggage cart with their belongings toward the elevator, stopping every few feet so the wasted couple could catch up to him. I sit on a couch and watch the bizarre pair. The bellhop has to put up with all their crap and chances are they won't have the wherewithal to leave him a tip. Then again, because their extreme intoxication, they probably can't make out Ben Franklins from pesos. Maybe they'll accidentally leave him a stack of hundreds, thinking they're handing him singles. I hope to God at that moment that I've never looked that bad on any number of pint-tipping, shot-gulping Friday nights.

The bellhop looks in my direction. I glance at the obnoxious guests, then steer my gaze back to the anxious worker. Good luck.

He returns to the lobby about ten minutes later, still shaking his head.

"I have a feeling that won't be the last time we hear from them tonight," he says.

I disagree. No one that drunk can remain awake for long, absent a few lines of coke or speed to keep them going.

"They'll be asleep in a few minutes," I say. "No way can they keep their eyes open much longer."

"Doubt it."

"Why do you say that?"

"The front desk manager said they've been here before. He told me that the flight completely freaks out these characters. They have to get bombed out of their skulls before they get on the plane, and the anxiety of the trip gets them so uptight that they'll probably keep drinking into the night. Room service is already on the way with a bottle of Bacardi."

"They won't even hear the waiter knocking at the door."

"We'll see."

As it turns out, the victim hadn't been attacked by a robber or by some sadistic assailant. She reveals that her husband was the perpetrator. When the cops arrive, she pleads with them not to arrest hubbie.

I escort the two uniformed officers upstairs, but it isn't necessary to tell them where the room is located; instead, they follow the trail of blood from the elevator to the crime scene, a corner suite at the end of the hall.

The door is open a crack. The officers draw their guns and hold them at their side. I follow them into the room, each of us glancing at the bathroom to the left, where lumped, coagulated blood is spread across the floor.

The woman has apparently hit her head—or had her head beaten—on the marble strip in the bathroom doorway. A pool of blood fills the cracks between several prices of ceramic tile, then gradually fades across the floor in a pattern of crimson dots.

The officers holster their weapons when they enter the bedroom. The husband is asleep under the covers, snoring loudly.

"Wake up, asshole," the first cop says.

The drunk stirs a bit. His deep-throated snores skip a few beats, while rising a few octaves. Cop number two takes it a step further, introducing himself by kicking *El Alcoholico* on the bottom of both feet.

It works.

The wife-beater, as squinty-eyed drunk as he is, spasms at the sight of the burly cops standing over him.

"Where eez my wife?" he asks.

I look over at the officers. We just stand there, disbelief written on our faces. This guy truly doesn't recall what has taken place.

The cop slowly leans down to the bed. He says nothing, but maintains eye contact with the increasingly squirming drunk. For a moment, all is quiet, with the exception of the air conditioner's low hum and assortment of metal gadgets on the cop's leather utility belt creaking and tapping. He says, calmly, "You put her in the hospital, you friggin idiot."

"Eez not true! Eez not true! Where eez my wife?" He tries pushing the cop away, but the officer grabs his arm and twists it behind his back. He nearly brings the Mexican's wrist to the back of his neck, and I reluctantly wait to hear a pop or a crack. I'm about to witness a cop snap somebody's arm. But what am I to do? Tell him to stop? With the image of the bloodied wife jumping into the elevator still fresh in my mind, I'm not much concerned for his well-being at the moment. I sigh with relief, however, when the officer lets go.

Perhaps the guy deserves to feel pain. Maybe it's necessary that someone inflict pain upon him—just as he had done to his wife—for the sake of simply getting through to him. Then again, it's probably better to let the system accomplish that task. A night spent in a foreign jail, for anyone, must be unnerving. And if this pampered, chubby rascal ends up in Riker's Island for the entire weekend, he's likely be shuddering his way back to Tijuana.

"Where eez my wife?" he continues. "Where eez my, where eez, where, where…"

His voice drifts off. Just as he had probably fallen asleep after smashing his wife's head in a drunken rage, he returns once again to dreamland.

"Let's go," the cop says. I mistakenly think he's telling the guy to get out of bed, figuring they're about to handcuff him. But he's talking to his partner and me. The show's over. Onto the next 9-1-1 call.

"Wait a second," I say. "Aren't you going to lock him up?"

"Can't."

"Why the hell not?"

"No complainant. His wife doesn't want to press charges. Besides, even if we did lock him up, he'd post bail, go back to Guadalajara or wherever the hell he's from, then never show up for court. Believe me, processing him would be a waste of everyone's time."

A lot of the craziness at the hotel stems from sheer drunkenness. Something about the setting that inspires people to consume mass quantities of alcohol and, to a lesser or at least a less obvious extent, drugs. Some guests get inebriated no doubt because they're on vacation and they're simply letting loose. Others are on business and want to escape from the grind of living out of suitcases and being far from their families. And still others, well, I guess they vote in favor of fun, however elusive it is when alcohol is inhaled like its oxygen. Unfortunately, that fun usually came at someone else's expense.

Get This Hoe Outta Here

For instance, take one group of frequent Palace guests—The Johnson Brothers—a gang of Kansas City hoodlums, I mean, nightclub owners. One glimpse and I know these characters are trouble. My first encounter is as non-confrontational as viewing, from the comfort of my living room, an early Hollywood satire of black gangster stereotypes. But rather than being devised by a couple of white guys safely laughing it up in the studio, this production is independently crafted, choreographed and put on public display by its actors.

The Johnson's and their crew descend on the hotel in a super-stretch limo, a freakish vehicle longer than a bus and displaying more extraneous lights than a cheesy 1950s depiction of a UFO. The first guy that emerges is wearing a form-fitting suit that cries out money, custom-made, to be certain. I'm talking about threads of the $2,000-plus variety.

I'm tempted to say he looks sharp, but for the fact that his outfit lacks a shirt. Oh, and he's also wearing a gold chain around his neck that may be thicker than the anchor chain on the Titanic.

Never before have I seen a gold chain that chunky. Even though it's likely to be hollow, this piece of jewelry is as cylindrical as a velvet rope hanging from a row of stanchions on the line going into a movie theater, no exaggeration. Real funky.

I know I risk sounding like an ignoramus trying to justify a racist reaction, but you'll have to take the word of this pen-wielding white-cracker. Born in the Bronx and raised in the multicultural New York City suburb of Lakewood, N.J., I claim expertise in differentiating between *gangstas* and plain ol' working-class black folk, who throughout my life have made up many of my friends, coworkers, high school football-team members and neighbors.

And the Johnson brothers and their buddies are far from plain.

A front-desk manager explains to me that the Johnsons own a nightclub in the Midwest. I've got no reason to think this is a lie. "Come on, they must be drug dealers," other coworkers say. Maybe they're right. Then again, it's also safe to assume that some of my fellow employees bolster their paychecks by selling drugs on the side. It's equally a foolish assumption without having evidence backing up such a claim.

The Johnsons always stay in the Towers, where they rent two adjacent suites on the 41st floor. I understand why they chose these two particular units. For one, they get an unobstructed view of the Empire State Building and the entire southern tip of Manhattan. But more importantly, no one is below them. The Fortieth floor contains nothing but machine rooms and ventilation equipment. They can stomp on the floors if they choose. Likewise, these deluxe chambers, replete with thirty foot long living rooms and crystal chandeliers, are situated between the southwest corner of the hotel on one side and a set of elevators on the other. No one underneath *or* adjacent to them. Not a soul to hear them. Sometimes you can hear a commotion in their rooms—loud conversations, laughing bordering on screaming, even late at night—but at least they have the courtesy, for lack of a better word, to keep their distance from the other guests.

Despite these measures, their mamas apparently failed to teach them not to beat the crap out of hookers and dump them in the hallway when they get sick of them.

For the most part, they're hardly ever in the building. If not for the fact that I'm working mainly on the midnight shift, I'd never see them. New York's clubs keep them occupied most of the night, and the Johnson crew sleeps half the day. And on the rare occasion that someone is situated close enough to them to complain about their boisterousness, the clique quiets down on request, no questions asked.

One night I approach their door in response to a noise complaint. I raise my hand, about to knock, then stop. I repeat the process, bending my knuckles in preparation for a loud series of taps on the door, but dropping my hand to my side, head tilted downward, wishing the situation didn't exist or would go away on its own.

Having subdued this fit of wishful thinking, I alert the Johnsons to my presence. Without hesitation they apologize for the disturbance.

"Here's something for your trouble," one of their underlings says. He opens the door just a crack to hand me a twenty-dollar bill. He's trying, unsuccessfully, to keep the cloud of pot smoke from creeping into the hallway. Not that I care that they're getting stoned, tip or no tip. I'm a house dick, not a cop. As far as I'm concerned it's not my business.

"Thank you, sir. Enjoy the rest of your evening," I say with a smile.

Too bad all noise complaints aren't so easily resolved.

They return a few months later for another four-day weekend. Although they don't know it, it's about to be their last one.

"House security, we just received a report of an assault taking place outside of room number forty-one twelve" the service operator's voice bellows through the speaker of my portable radio. "Would you like me to call 9-1-1?"

"I'll investigate first, operator."

I call for backup, but none comes. Although we typically have four house officers on duty for each shift, one had called out sick that night and the other two were in the hotel taking their breaks. Not coffee breaks, mind you, but naps. Not that this is a surprise. This is standard albeit unwritten procedure that's at the heart of the game on midnights, the graveyard shift, as most people call it. More on this later When I arrive at the Forty-First floor—even before I exit the elevator—I hear a series of loud *thwacks*, the unmistakable sound of someone getting walloped in the head. It corresponds with a woman pleading with someone to let her go. The voices are traveling from the south end of the floor, right outside the Johnson's suites. I pause, listening to further assess the situation before jumping into the middle. I know from experience that these guys are into drugs and prostitution. In fact, earlier in the night, about a half dozen hookers pay them a visit.

My backup still hasn't arrived, so I hesitate intervening. I'm not about to die for whatever this woman has gotten herself into.

"You shouldn't have done that, bitch," I hear from around the corner. *Thwack*. Then another *thwack thwack*.

"Stop it, you're hurting me!" she shouts. "I'm telling you, I don't have it." She never once screams for help. She's too busy denying that she he has something, whatever *it* is.

It sounds like the guy is roughing her up. I step into the hallway and make my presence known.

"House security!" I announce as I turn the corner. The tough-guy routine usually works wonders with most people. The confidence needed to imply that you'll put a hurting on someone for being uncooperative is one of the reasons I rarely have to get physical.

The *threat* of force typically helped to avoid the *use* of force. But in this case, I'm outmatched.

Stepping into the hallway, I meet a hulking homey that makes me look small. He's like the Kingpin, Spiderman's archenemy, a character who's nearly as wide as he's tall. He's of the sort that doesn't move when you hit him. Trying to give one of those "we can do this hard way or the easy way" speeches is going to be a waste of time, if not just downright hazardous to my health.

He looks me right in the eye, as if daring me to come forward. He then lays his right paw against the side of the woman's head. *Thwack!* An earring rolls across the floor and nearly lands at my feet.

"That hoe stole my shit," he says to me, *shouts at me.* "Get her out of here before I throw her out the window!"

I'm not about to call his bluff. He has the potential to throw us both out of the window. Better to let him ease his way back into the room.

Sorry, lady, but they don't pay me enough to die for you.

She's putting up with all that smacking while never shedding a tear, further confirming my suspicions that she's a hooker. (I'll explain in a later chapter how I could nearly smell prostitutes, figuratively speaking).

I pick up the earring and hand it to her. Despite being smacked around by the Black Kingpin, she isn't bleeding or bruised.

"Do you need a doctor?" I ask.

"No, I'll manage," she says, fixing her hair.

"Do you want to sign a complaint against that guy? I can call the cops, if you want to."

She purses her lips and glares at me from the corner of her eye for a few motionless seconds. Yeah, I know the deal at this point. Short of getting beaten into mush with a pipe, most streetwalkers want nothing to do with the police. When they have a gripe with a customer, they send over some goon from the escort service to conduct a readjustment of the bill—or of the guy's face. Cops are a no-no, unless they work for a whorehouse on the side.

"Do you want me to get you a cab?"

"I'd appreciate that."

We ride the elevator downstairs in silence. No doubt she's afraid I'm going to question whether she ripped off Brother Johnson.

Although maybe she's gained cash or a watch or some other valuable, the likely throbbing in her skull is reminding her of the cost of conducting such business. I figure there's no need to push the issue with a verbal probe. I escort her out of the hotel and hail a cab, never to see her or the Johnsons ever again.

Despite the tens of thousands of dollars the crew spends at the Palace every year, hotel management bans them for life, understandably so. It just isn't worth tarnishing the hotel's image and taking the chance of driving away even more business that the Johnsons ever could give to the Palace.

Such calls on the midnight shift don't always involve an element of fear. In fact, the next *distress* call is nothing less than a treat.

Champagne Jam

This time, the woman in distress is the temporary neighbor of a young couple living it up one night at her expense. She demands to speak directly with someone from security, the service operator advises me.

The guest, a skinny woman in her early forties draped in frumpy pajamas, opens the door to her room. A sneer rests on her face like a bird incubating an egg. You know her expression is there to stay. She stands without saying a word, as if I should have already guessed why she was so angry.

"Well, do you hear that racket?" she asks.

I listen, leaning closer to her neighbor's room. Nothing but the sound of the elevator further down the hallway.

"Uh, what racket?" I ask with a hint of annoyance.

"You don't hear that? Those idiots next door have been having sex all night at my expense!"

"So waddaya want me to do? Tell them have quieter sex?"

"Tell them to put their pajamas on and go to sleep! This is hotel, not a whorehouse!"

She takes a step toward me, then asks with seriousness, "Surely you don't expect me to listen to them rolling around in bed all night, do you?"

I stare at her without saying a word. A hotel indeed resembles a whorehouse, as far as I can tell. What the hell is she talking about? I fight the urge to say, 'You need to get laid, lady.'

"Well if you don't do something about that, that, that," pausing for a second before blurting, "that loud, obnoxious slut in 1222, then I will!" She starts marching toward the other room. I urge her to reconsider.

"Wait a second ma'am," I ask politely, delaying her while thinking of what to say next. "Please go back inside your room. I will, hmm, let's see. I'll call them on the phone instead of confronting them, okay? I'll take care of it."

Loud sex? Give me a break. I get the impression she isn't so mad about them being loud as she's angry that they're having fun while she isn't. I decide to call the front desk manager and let her deal with it. Calming an unattractive, sex-starved woman just isn't in my job description.

Yolanda meets me near the room in question. "Hey, thanks, Yolanda. I'll see you later," I say as I try walking away. She squints, revealing disapproval, then shakes her head and motions with her finger to return. "Uh-uh. Get back here."

She walks up to room twelve twenty-two, where I can now hear a young woman giggling and carrying on. Yolanda knocks on the door and says to me, "Nice try, by the way."

A bellhop arrives at the room with a luggage cart. "I called the guests before I came up here," Yolanda says. "They've agreed to move to another room. You can stick around to make sure there's no trouble." She then gets on the elevator and goes back downstairs.

When the guest opens the door, I realize how fortunate I am that it works out that way.

A beautiful young woman, probably no older than twenty, stands there smiling, wrapped only in a towel.

"Hi, come on in!" she says with a bounce. She starts to wobble back into the room and takes two or three steps before the towel falls off. She has a spectacular body, a lean, sculpted physique, with skin smooth and blemish-free, near-perfect in that sense, like an airbrushed photo of a model gracing the cover of Cosmopolitan. No signs of sagging anywhere.

Her male acquaintance, drunker than she, also greets us. He's still in bed, under the covers and propped up by a stack of pillows. A smirk creeps up the left side of his mouth. He raises one eyebrow in concert with the twisted half-smile, as if gravity is working in reverse, yanking half his head toward the ceiling. Despite his inebriation, he's cordial, although a hint of condescension hides beneath the surface of his politeness.

His tone sends the message: Retrieve my bags, poor slobs, for I soon shall be naked with a woman you are lusting over but can only touch in your dreams.

The thought, however absurd, that I have a shot at stealing away his woman, adds to my dislike of this drunken clown. He's vulnerable, like a fish in a barrel, just waiting to be eliminated from contention. He can't possibly have the stamina to suit the physical needs of the young beauty in our presence.

The room is littered with boxes and bags from Saks, Bloomingdales and other high-end Manhattan shops.

"I see you did a little shopping," I say.

"I sure did," she replies. "Want to see what I bought?"

Before I can respond, there's another knock at the door. I look through the peephole. It's a waiter holding a tray with a silver bucket of ice, a bottle of Dom Perignon resting on top.

"Did you order something?" I ask before offering to open the door.

"Is it room service?" Knees bent, body frozen, she's posed like a linebacker waiting for the quarterback to say, "Hike!"

I open the door for her to see.

"Oh, goody!" she says, jumping in the air. A couple of bounces later, her towel falls to the floor once more. "Oops." She leans forward to pick it up. Her breasts shift downward and sway toward us. Mammalian protuberances, as Frank Zappa used to say, with their gravity induced length revealed, center stage. Yep, she's putting on a show. And I'm taking in every second of it, despite being teased like a puppy whose master displays a treat and laughs as he pulls it away.

Each employee stands still, eyebrows raised, mouths agape. The waiter fumbles with the bottle of Dom as he's unexpectedly greeted at the door by a pair of jiggling boobs.

The waiter pops the cork, pours two glasses and quickly exits.

"Care to join us?" the girl asks as she tilts her head in our direction, eyes squinted and unblinking, as if making an offer that we won't dare to reject.

The bellhop tries to answer first, saying "Steve, I think we better get…"

"We would love to join you!" I say, cutting him off. I shoot a glance at him, a not-so-subtle hint that we're staying put. The female guest brings back two extra glasses and fills them, unaware the champagne is bubbling over the rim and spilling on the floor.

"Enjoy," she says as she extends her hand. No doubt I will. The bellhop, on the other hand, fakes a sip, puts the glass down and starts loading bags onto the luggage cart.

The woman inspects the bottle, now half-empty, and decides to order more. Meanwhile, my coworker begins delivering her belongings to the other room, down the hallway. He makes two trips to accommodate the volume of shopping bags and luggage. By time he's done room service arrives with another bottle of champagne, eliciting another round of cheerleader-style kicks and arm-motions from the young guest.

And of course, the towel falls off again. I take another gulp of Dom, emptying my glass. Seeing this, she runs over to me with the bottle for another round.

Only this time, she forgets to put the towel back on, much to the dismay of her mate, whom by this time I realize is a nobody in her eyes. Just another dude she's met while carousing New York with her daddy's Amex card in hand. This chump isn't happy with the situation, but doesn't have the gumption to complain. Any man unwilling to address such an issue is unworthy to be in this woman's presence, I reason. As the quick succession of drinks starts swimming in my head, my blood pressure rises and makers me more contemptuous of the pathetic fat bastard, who's still lying in bed like a chubby little Roman emperor waiting for a servant to feed him grapes.

The urge to drag this guy out of bed and toss him into the hallway, simply for the crime of not having the balls to take control, is an attractive alternative—or so I think. The combined effect of the buzz in my brain, the elusiveness of the young hottie before me and my growing scorn for her pseudo companion clouds my thinking. Somehow I muster up enough sense to remind myself of the inebriated state I'm in plus the fact the time clock is ticking. I discard the nutty ideas brewing in my skull. It's bad enough that I've been partying in front of other hotel workers, who by now had already moved us to the other room and fled the scene, but to launch hostilities with a guest?

A waiter arrives with a third bottle of Dom. At this point, Slim climbs back under the covers, alone. Finally, he tires of my unwillingness to leave voluntarily.

"Don't you have something else to do?" he asks.

"Not a thing," I say. "Not a damn thing."

I'm getting impatient that *he* isn't taking a hint and leaving *me* alone with the girl. Although I manage to keep my hostile attitude at bay, I'm convinced that the young beauty wants this guy to leave. She just doesn't know how to break it him. I'm tempted to give her suggestions, but I relent.

She prances around the room as she recounts her shopping adventure. She even runs into the bathroom to try on a few outfits for me. Not for her temporary mate, but *me*. I'm heartened by the personalized attention she's giving me. Some guys spend hundreds of dollars for such entertainment—and from infinitely less attractive women in dingy quarters, no less. And here I am in one of New York's top luxury hotels playing voyeur with an intermittently nude 20-year-old—and getting paid for it. What a racket.

This Isn't What You Think It Might Be

Nearly as revealing but infinitely less appealing is a meeting I have with The Accidental Streaker.

I'm patrolling the hotel basement, a jumble of housekeeping offices, storerooms and a thirty-five person-capacity cafeteria that Leona provides for the hotel's thousand or so employees. It's around three a.m. No too much activity, other than employees snoring from makeshift beds arranged wherever they can find space. I'm wandering, killing time before my three-hour break begins.

I turn the corner and nearly bump into someone, reflexively apologizing for not paying attention but before realizing that it's a stranger, obviously not an employee. I stress he *obviously* isn't an employee for one glaring reason: he's naked.

We each flinch, then freeze, remaining silent for several seconds, uncertain of one another's next move. I step back, poised to swing a forearm under his jaw to incapacitate him if necessary. Can't tell if he's an escaped mental patient, passive or violent, or just a pervert.

He's trying to cover his crotch with a fluorescent orange bag that reads, ironically, in big black letters, F-I-R-E H-O-S-E. You can find hoses on every emergency stairway landing on both the north and south sides of the building. Each is loosely wrapped with such a glow-in-the-dark cover. Well, except for one.

He steps from side to side, unsure what to say, like a child refusing to admit that he has to pee.

"This isn't what you think it might be," he blurts out.

I pause, waiting for an answer. He struggles to find the right words while continuing to shift weight from one foot to the other.

"Explain yourself quickly or I'm calling the cops," I say. "I think you've got some explaining to do. You've got five seconds."

"I got locked out of my room."

"Yeah, right." I reach for my radio to call for backup. "I'll leave that for the police to decide."

"That won't be necessary," he says as he steps toward me, as if ready to grab the radio out of my hand.

"You better step back, or I'm gonna deck you," I say. "Do you understand?"

Distance appears between us.

"I'm quite serious," he says. "If you bring me to my room I will gladly show you identification. My wallet is on the dresser, next to the phone."

Luckily for him we're near the housekeeping office. A pile of bathrobes are nearby. I grab one and throw it to him. Better to lessen his humiliation, just in case he's legit, as he claims.

"Here, cover yourself. I'm gonna call upstairs and make sure you're not full of baloney. I hope you understand."

"I'd be disappointed if you didn't confirm my identity."

I'm still thinking he's full of crap, but I plow onward. He utters a name, which I assume he's making up. I pick up a house phone to call the front desk, bracing myself in the event he lashes out when I uncover his lies.

But the name matches.

"Okay, sir, I'm gonna take you upstairs," I say. "Even though I confirmed the name you gave me, I don't think it's asking to much to show me a picture ID." He nods in agreement as we go into the elevator.

I want to apologize for being so abrupt, but I keep quiet. He's got to understand my initial hostility. After all, he's in the basement without any clothes, in the wee hours of the morning.

I call one of my colleagues, Mickey, and ask him to meet me by the ground-floor elevators, quickly.

"Bring a master key with you," I say.

There's no immediate response.

"Peacock, what's going on?" the tinny voice on the radio says.

"Do me a favor, just meet me where I asked you to. I'll explain later."

I look across the elevator at the partly clothed stranger, realizing that this is going to look weird to my coworkers. There I am, standing in the elevator with some half-naked guy—and I'm asking my colleague for access to a room. The elevator door opens. No other guests are around. *But then there's Mickey*, who's forcing himself to blink, mouth open, as if unable to speak.

"I'll be down in a minute," I say sternly as he hands me the key.

"Hey, no problem," he says. He glances back and forth at the two of us, a smile suddenly emerging as he says, "Hey, take your time." The compartment whisks me away with the accidental streaker. We look away, saying nothing, as

Mickey's laughter spills through the door into the elevator shaft, following us upward and fading with each passing floor.

I open the room door and peek around, making sure there are no unanticipated surprises waiting. Mr. Fire Hose walks in after me. As promised, the wallet is on a night table, hidden behind the phone, to the left of the bed. He show me his driver's license and I thank him, exiting without further comment.

As I'm about to leave, however, I realize that one question does indeed have to be asked.

"By the way, sir," I say, biting my bottom lip and hesitantly looking away. "How in the world did you end up outside your room, you know, naked and all?"

He flutters his eyelids and presses his lips together on one side of his face, as if resisting the urge to smile. He doesn't respond. I wait. Sensing that I expect an answer, he says, "It's a long story," then slams the door. He isn't obligated to say another word, and knows it.

Returning to the office to write an incident report, I continue wondering what the hell this guy had gotten himself into. I mean, why would he even consider opening the door—never mind going into the hallway—without any clothes, even for a second?

Was he flashing other guests? Not possible. We would've gotten a complaint or two on *that* one. Did he decide to take a stroll down the hallway nude, knowing that most guests were sleeping, thereby enabling him to enjoy a sense of freedom that 'normal' folk typically don't pursue?

The answer is unknown. My list of possibilities needs a mental burial, fast.

Sambuca, Anyone?

Some guests simply are in their own worlds, actions unpredictable and unexplainable. You see, when I deal with the seemingly nutty ones, they end up elegant and well-mannered. Then when I expect normalcy, the outcome falls in the bizarre category.

Take the Spumonis and the Goldbergs, for instance, the families of two guests—one Jewish, the other Italian—who held their wedding reception in the Versailles Ballroom. Although it's common for Jews and Catholics to marry, in the eyes of most in-laws and aunts and uncles and cousins, the arrangement is as mixable as oil and water.

Nevertheless, it's a civil event, despite the question of whether the families accept the pair's religious differences. Civil, that is, until they run out of Sambuca.

The Italian side downs a few liters of the imported, high-test licorice-flavored liqueur. They want more. I don't know if the hotel has run out of the sweet liquid or if the wedding party exceeded their quota (despite the $25,000 nightly price tag for the room rental). But the Goldbergs are paying the bill. They refuse to cough up the cash for more Sambuca, much to the heartbreak of the Spumonis.

An all-out brawl is the by-product of that dispute, fists flying and tables upended. Fortunately it's resolved before we call the police. That's all we need is a bunch of New York City cops to come in and rough up our guests, rightly or wrongly. Don't get me wrong, the officers from NYPD's Midtown North precinct are helpful to us over the years. But who could blame them if they were to end up smacking around a bunch of hardheaded, wealthy partygoers who are throwing empty Sambuca bottles at one another?

John Gotti Jr., son of the then- soon-to-be-imprisoned Mafia boss, also held his wedding reception in the ballroom. But unlike the Spumonis and the Goldbergs, John Gotti and company were on best behavior. No fights, no harassing of guests. Just another well-run, ostentatious event at the Versailles.

Of course, a cast of characters straight out of *The Sopranos* lined the area surrounding the ballroom. Even nosy photojournalists who are otherwise determined to make a quick buck didn't dare violate that gauntlet of *goombahs*, as they're known in New York. Someone from the Gotti crew advised the hotel security chief to just keep the house dicks away. There were enough of gorillas in stereotypical flashy suits and poorly matched ties to provide the event with all the security they needed. No need to tell us twice about that request.

The event ran without a hitch.

I'll Pay You To…Protect Me

At the start of a midnight shift I learn that a female guest in the Towers needs to speak with someone from security. Supposedly it's urgent, but not an emergency. I picture some rich babe in need of assistance, a damsel in distress desiring immediate attention.

Maybe I'll get lucky tonight. If nothing else, I'll at least get a tip out of it—not an unreasonable expectation when dealing with those in the Towers. Guests regularly throw us a bone, a ten or twenty here and there, even an occasional hundred.

As she opens the door to her suite, a tip is no doubt forthcoming. Two of them, in fact.

A woman in her sixties poses in the doorway—left hand on her hip, right hand stretched out high against the wall—her giant, sagging breasts pointing at me, or should I say, *at my feet*. I don't mean to sound full of myself, but for her, my arrival is a dream come true. Her wandering eyes confirm that assumption. She inspects me from my hair to my shoes, with a laser beam focus below the belt.

This isn't the princess I had envisioned, although in a sense she was definitely in distress.

"What can I do for you ma'am?" I ask. I squint as if in pain, realizing how mistaken I am to ask such a question.

She smiles. "Perhaps you can help me. I am in fear of the man in the room next door. I need extra security to ensure my safety."

She claims to be uncomfortable having connecting door linking the two suites. I tell her that both are always locked, unless someone rents the two units simultaneously and requests that they be opened.

The guy in the adjacent room is a threat, she insists, although she doesn't try to justify this claim. You've got nothing to fear, I want to tell her, because if he breaks into your place and catches a glimpse of what I'm now viewing, he'll faint, run away or jump out the window. Pick one.

I'm guessing the room next door might even be vacant. The way she repeatedly scans the length of my mid-section, there's no question which chamber (hers) is empty and needs filling. A chill runs down my spine at the thought.

This woman must be deluded. The combination of her wandering eyes and sex-toy-store variety of clothing suggest that she's confident at having at least a long shot at seducing me. I offer to have a bellhop escort her to another room, where she would feel safer, before she comes right out and says what's really on her mind. Of course, *this* will jeopardize the safety of the unfortunate bellhop that ends up escorting her to the other room, but that's not my concern. I have to make the offer for the sake of courtesy. More importantly, it's critical that I wiggle my way out of this situation without offending her.

"I have a better idea," she says. "It would be quite inconvenient to move all of my belongings in the middle of the night." She hesitates, then presses an incisor into her lower lip before saying, "I would like to pay you to stay with me for the evening, in order to, well, protect me."

She waits for an answer, while restoring visual focus at my belt line.

I've heard about such offers to employees, but dismissed such stories as fantasies dreamt up by fellow workers. Just blue collar dudes imagining wealthy guests paying them for, or even demanding, sex. One guy from engineering told me that a female guest begged him to bang her over the bathroom sink after he fixed it—even though her husband was in the room!

"Oh, he's sound asleep. Come on, he won't hear a thing," she supposedly told him.

In light of my current situation, I belatedly realize he was telling the truth.

I apologize to the woman for being unable to provide the requested 'service.'

"We patrol the building twenty-four hours a day," I tell her. "I'll inform the other house officers to pay attention to the room next door to you. That's the best I can do."

Unwilling to retreat, she lunges at me as I walk away, immediately catching herself before making contact. Her hand covers her mouth, as if she's finally embarrassed by her actions.

"Wait! Maybe one of your other men would like to protect me," she says. Whether consciously or absentmindedly, she grabs the front of her nightie at waist level, causing the silky material to press against her flesh, thereby making her dark nipples more visible. Nothing seems to dissuade her. Not shame, not even rejection. It's an understatement to say she's in denial. Then again, maybe her persistence is the result of past experience. At some point in her travels, she probably succeeds in getting a lay out of a young, willing employee. After all, some people will do anything for the right price.

It isn't until the next day that it sinks in just *how* old this woman really is. In the middle of a high society/gossip section in one of the local newspapers is a picture of the horny guest, posing with the late actor George Burns, who I vaguely remember was celebrating his 90th birthday at the time. She's hanging on him as if they're good old buddies. It's feasible that a photographer had showed up at their high school reunion.

Crusty Santa

Extremes of *everything*, it seemed, are commonplace at the Palace. Extremes of waste. Extremes of pleasure-seeking. Extremes between the wealth-laden Palace guests and the street people who wander into the hotel. At any given moment I'm dealing with well-dressed, powerful people, and within seconds I turn around and encounter the emotionally disturbed coming into the hotel from the street.

On the other hand, at any time I might find myself dealing with people exhibiting a combination of those attributes: simultaneously well dressed *and* mentally ill (or at the very least, *bizarre*) and powerful insofar as they were privileged hotel guests.

At peak checkout time one morning, an older couple draped in filthy, tattered clothing walks into the packed lobby. Those who don't catch a glimpse of the pair smell them soon after. I rush over with the intention of ejecting them, but they quickly split up. The female heads toward the front desk. The man ventures deeper into the lobby, hovering near the elevators. We've got a situation.

Before I can intercept the burly, bearded man, he plops down on one of two couches located on either side of the main staircase. His body odor permeates the air. He looks and smells like a ragged Santa Claus that climbed down a few sewer holes instead of chimneys.

"Can I help you, sir?" I ask, my impatient tone revealing a lack of sincerity in the question.

"No thank you," he responds in an Australian accent, eager to claim that his wife is taking care of business at the registration desk.

Here's a guy with an aroma that rivals a stray dog, and yet he can look me in the eye and tell me he's a guest. This is going to be interesting.

I motion for him to come with me as I walk toward the front desk.

"Yeah, okay. Your wife's checking you in, uh-huh. Why don't we see how she's doing?"

His smile disappears. Now he's puzzled and annoyed.

"No," he said emphatically, stretching out the 'o' for an extra couple of seconds. "I'm quite comfortable here."

I step closer, ready to grab him by the arm and lead him out the door. "Come on. Really, sir. It's time to take a walk."

"A walk? No walks for me. I'm exhausted. What a long flight."

Crusty Santa, as I silently refer to him, is beginning to test my patience. At first his routine is cute, amusing, but now other guests are nearby, watching my every move. I'm sure they want the smelly fellow taken away quickly, but stench or no stench, I hesitate getting rough—trespasser or not, he's about 50 years my senior. I can't win. I decide that I'll let him permanently stink up the couch and the whole damn lobby rather than manhandle the old timer.

A new approach is warranted. I lean down, inches from his face, and say in a low-pitched, angry tone, "Well, sir, it's time for you to…"

He cut me off in mid-sentence, pointing beyond me.

"Here they come now!"

What is he trying to pull? I refuse to look over my shoulder. If I take my eye off of him, he might kick me or take a swing. He abruptly stands from his seat, and I get in a defensive position in case he puts his head down and charges me like a bull.

From behind me I hear a lady say, "Are you ready, dear?" The guy's partner-in-crime, as I mistakenly assumed she was, is standing next to a bellhop, a stack of luggage on a cart by his side.

"G'day," Crusty Santa says to me in trademark Aussie fashion. The bellhop escorts him and his wife to the elevator. He turns his head in my direction and nods. All is forgiven.

They Even Found Me In Hartford

The fire alarm is activated throughout the building. It's about two in the morning. Guests come streaming down the stairs. Some are in a near-panic, despite my assurances that, as it turns out, it's a false alarm.

No fire, no smoke, we apologize for the inconvenience. *Please return to your rooms*, I announce.

They file into the elevators. All but one, that is. She emerges from the middle of the disappearing crowd. And as the last of the other guests departs, this young woman—wearing only a bathrobe, not including a towel that's wrapped around her head—stands silently, watching me.

The beauty mask caked on her face accentuates a set of troubled eyes—her mouth is shut, but the windows into her mind are open for all to see.

The blue-faced woman approaches, looking over her shoulder every few steps.

"Excuse me," she whispers. "I think I know why the alarm went off."

A confession appears to be forthcoming.

"This may sound strange to you, but I assure you that what I'm about to say is true."

Having heard that, now I know I'm in for a treat.

"Yes, go ahead."

"They pulled the alarm to harass me, not the rest of the people staying here."

"They?"

"Yes, *they*."

"And who may *they* be?"

"A group of men have been following me around the country, pulling the fire alarm everywhere I go, just to deprive me of sleep."

Our eyes are locked in a stare, but for several seconds neither of us speaks.

Uncomfortable with the silence, she says, "Well, I told you it might sound strange."

"Might?" I ask with a chuckle, finding it hard to restrain myself. Yeah, it's strange, all right, even for New York standards.

47

"You have my assurances it's true. No matter where I have gone, whether it's been Los Angeles, Minneapolis or Houston, they have discovered where I'm staying."

She pauses, then takes another look behind her. Returning to a whisper, she says, "*They even found me in Hartford, Connecticut.*"

What do you say in response to such a statement? Simply wish her a good night, then walk away, that's what.

"No, please listen to me!" she begs with eyes shut and fists clenched, arms bent at the elbows, pumping up and down in a series of slow and steady motions.

She's having delusions, no doubt. I don't lack empathy for her state of confusion. Then again, she's a potential danger to myself and to the hotel's occupants. One doesn't have to be a psychiatrist to see she suffering from paranoia.

I imagine another guest getting on the elevator with her and suddenly she thinks they're one of her alleged stalkers. That's the kind of situation that makes headlines. I picture the New York Post, infamous for front-page attention-grabbers such as *Headless Body Found in Topless Bar*, with a headline like: *Wealthy Wacko Guts Guard*.

Wanting to put her mind at ease, if that's at all possible at this point, I tell her that the security staff will increase its patrols to see to it that no one interrupts her sleep.

"What room are you in? I'll make sure we check your floor regularly throughout the night," I say.

She's appreciative of the offer, unaware it's a lie

It turns out that she's staying in room fifty ten, in the Palace Towers. There are only top-of-the-line luxury suites on the fiftieth floor, none that cost less than $750 per night. I later check the guest registry at the front desk. She has reservations for another two weeks. That's a lot of cash coming from a lost young lady with a poor perception of reality. And a lot of time for an unstable guest to be floating around the place awaiting the arrival of her perceived aggressors.

As ol' blue face walks toward the Tower elevators, I make one more mistake.

"By the way," I ask, "who are these men that keep following you?"

Without hesitation, she says, "Cuban gun-runners and cult members from the South," then gets on the elevator, repeatedly poking her head out before allowing the doors to close.

Cheap Ties and D-Cups

The Palace at certain times of the year nearly is filled to capacity. Except for rooms that they're preparing for occupancy, each of the thousand-plus units simultaneously teem with activity. So active, in fact, that the constant influx of people coming and going interferes with one's ability to catch get an elevator to his or her floor.

On one such night I need an elevator—quickly—to respond to a guest call. I approach the elevator bank on the ground floor as a dozen guests get out, slowing me down from getting into the next available compartment, which three other people enter. The doors nearly shut in my face, but I wave my hand between them, triggering the mirror-like metal panels to reopen.

The two tall-haired, big-busted women inside the compartment are not in the mood for waiting either.

These *Studio 54*-rejects cling to a guy wearing a nondescript, tan suit with a shirt unbuttoned down to his protruding belly. The opening in his polyester apparel reveals, unfortunately, an array of rope chains and gaudy, gold charms sitting on a bed of chest hair that he must have fertilized with Miracle Grow. Also, you could see that the girls, one blonde, the other brunette, had used an obscene amount of hair spray to make their mops stand so tall. Only in retrospect can I now say the scene screamed out, "1980s!"

The male is oblivious to my presence. No wonder, I guess, considering he has a couple of pairs of D-cups pressing against him. Both women, on the other hand, stare me down, the emerging snarls on their faces interfering with their ability to process their respective wads of Bubbleicious. Taking a break from arousing her companion, the brunette launches a verbal assault.

"Who the hell said you could get on this elevator with us?" she asks.

Then the blonde chimes in, pursing her lips in disgust then asking, "Where did you get such a cheap-looking tie?"

I glance over at Don Juan, figuring he has something to say as well.

He asks, "You're from security, right?"

Taking a peak at the radio in my hand, I nod hesitantly, preparing for another heaping of abuse. Surprisingly, he turns his attention to his low-class companions, grabs them both by the arm and half-seriously scolds them.

"You see this guy here? Do you see him? He's *The Man* in this building, you know what I mean? He's keeping an eye on things while we sleep, and I don't want you busting his balls, understand?"

They pull back slightly, their faces tensing up as if in mild shock. He shrugs his shoulders, smiling awkwardly, as if providing silent reassurance that he's only jesting. He reaches around their backs and grabs them both by the derriere, pulling them in tight so their breasts squash against him, to the point of nearly popping the appendages out of their dresses, in fact. He leans his head back and shuts his eyes, releasing a throaty groan that's dripping with lust, reeking of narcissism. Decadent pleasure is the sole item remaining on his agenda for the evening.

He pauses and wishes me a good night as I stop at the twentieth floor. How heartening it is that he's polite, although I'd prefer that he slips me a twenty for putting up with such nonsense.

Well, at least he's silenced the two obnoxious wenches. I'm thankful.

Louie, Louie

Such flaunting of material and physical possessions is, at times, like a kick in the head, but is less damaging to the psyche than the blatantly harsh treatment some guests heaped on the hired help. Under the circumstances, there are almost zero choices in responding to obnoxious, arrogant people. But occasionally, an employee experiences one of those special moments, when condescending behavior blows up in someone's face.

You don't have to lift a finger to cause it. Don't even have to raise your voice to cause such guests to self-destruct.

A cocktail waitress from Harry's escorts a young, meticulously dressed couple to a booth. It's a dark, cozy corner in Harry's, set back from the bar and away from most activity—the same spot where you occasionally see Brooke Shields sipping a glass of Perrier. Unlike the visibility of sitting at the bar, the booths enable visitors to impress their dates in private.

The male barks his order: "Get two glasses of the most expensive cognac in the house."

"Right away, sir," the waitress responds, "but just so you know…"

He cuts her off in mid-sentence, bellowing, "I didn't ask you for an explanation, just get the damn things!"

"If you say so."

She brings back two glasses of King Louis the XIII cognac—the finest cognac available, as requested—and, smiling like a pro, sets them on the table. The couple polishes off the first two glasses. Macho man then snaps his fingers. Get us another round, he says.

After a third round of drinks he asks for the check. The waitress adds up the total and places the bill on the table.

"Whenever you're ready, sir."

As she walks away, she hears, "Wait a damn minute!"

She returns to the booth, and he continues, "This must be a mistake. The total is over four hundred dollars We only had six drinks!"

"Well, sir, I was trying to tell you that our most expensive cognac is seventy dollars a glass. If you had let me finish what I was saying, you would have been aware of that."

She pauses for a moment, savoring her victory before asking matter-of-factly, "Will that be cash or charge?"

Damn New Yorkers

It isn't often that hotel guests become abusive. Yet, every so often, I can count on someone to take out his or her frustrations on me.

A stretch limo pulls up to the curb and an inebriated middle-aged couple opens their door before their driver reaches them. Upon speaking, the couple effortlessly reveals they're rednecks.

"Could y'all tell me where the hell an Italian restaurant called 'Il Tremino' or something stupid like that might be?" he asks. "My damn driver ain't got the slightest idea where it is."

"Come inside if you'd like," I say. "I'm not exactly sure where this place is, sir, but I'll check the listing at the bell captain's desk."

"That's mighty kind o' you, son."

I flip through the pages looking for this restaurant, whose name I didn't recognize. This guy is so far gone, I assume that 'Il Tremino' is just the first Italian-sounding word that pops into his brain. Up to this point he's pleasant, so I press onward to help him out. He mumbles the name of a street, which likewise is part of his drunken and illogical repertoire. Scanning the city guide, I try to narrow it down to an approximate location—not an easy task considering there are thousands upon thousands of restaurants in the city. I check the neighborhood-by-neighborhood listing. I look through "East Side-Mid-Town." Nothing. "West Side-Mid-Town." Still nothing.

The couple seems intent on getting to this place, so I ungrudgingly continue the search.

Breaking the relative silence in the lobby, the wobbly Slim Pickens look-alike suddenly says, "What the fuck is taking you so long?"

I drop the directory on the marble counter. *Nah, he couldn't possibly be talking to me*, I'm thinking. I look over my shoulder, hoping he's directing this anger at somebody else, anybody but me. He sees me glancing in his direction.

"That's right. I'm talkin' to you. What the fuck is takin' you so long?"

Oh my God, not today, I pray. This guy has a serious timing problem; he happens to be picking someone to mess with who's testifying in court that very week in a lengthy and stressful trial. That someone is *me*. And I'm not feeling stable, with or without unsolicited provocation.

The reason I was on edge? One year earlier, when I had temporarily left the Palace to become a New York City Special Patrolman on Roosevelt Island, I had been shot in the left armpit during a traffic stop. A retired cop, who later claimed I had harassed him and violated his civil rights, had blasted me at point-blank range with a .38 snub-nose revolver. The bullet had ripped through my body, narrowly missing a major artery as well as my lung. I had approached him for ignoring a red-metal octagonal plate containing the bright white letters S-T-O-P, which happened to be alongside a crosswalk in front of an elementary school. But technically, he didn't go through a stop sign, since it was never formally registered with the state Department of Transportation. Legally, the red octagon may as well have had a smiley face on it instead of the word 'stop.' The trial revealed he was no more obligated to halt than he was to smile.

Then during an early stage of the proceedings—in fact, the day before I faced Jethro in the hotel lobby—the judge ruled that someone, unknown to me, had intentionally destroyed the Public Safety Department's audiotape of all radio transmissions made before, during and after the near-fatal incident.

And there I am, after midnight, being tormented by some drunken hillbilly, while suffering from post-traumatic stress and becoming increasingly anxious about my unraveling court case. I'm near insanity, and this buffoon before me has no idea that he's provoking one of the most potentially dangerous people to mess with in all of midtown Manhattan.

"I go out of my way for you, and this is the thanks that I get?" I ask, the blood rushing so quickly to my head that I feel like I'm on the verge of a stroke.

"You Got-damn New Yorkers don't know shit about your own city! I'm tired of dealin' with you stupid sons o' bitches!" he says.

We stare at each other, quietly, for a few awkward seconds.

Although my voice is quivering, I find within myself a surprising ability to stay calm, asking, "Are you staying here at the hotel, sir?"

"No I'm not stayin' at this hotel ya sum bitch! An' you can be sure that this is the last time I evah…"

His acknowledgment that he's not a Palace guest changes the terms of debate. Realizing I no longer had to tolerate such abuse—after all, he isn't a registered guest, and therefore I have no obligation to cater to him—I nearly lose control.

I march toward him, fists unconsciously clenched at my side, eyes bulging and nostrils flaring.

He wakes up.

"I'm sorry, son," he says. "I just had a little too much to drink this evenin'."
He stammers, then asks uncomfortably, "Wontcha shake my hand?"

I raise my hands for a second, and retreat to the other end of the lobby. But the fool insists on following me, apologizing as he does so. I want so badly to shake him violently, but internally something holds me back.

Words pour from my mouth a few monotone syllables at a time, but increasing in pace and in volume.

"I suggest…that you go back…to Kentucky…or where ever you came from!" So loud is my command that I endure a burning sensation in my lungs and throat.

Growling like a pit bull, wide-eyed and without blinking, I advance on him. He takes a few steps backwards to get away. He fumbles for words. Unable to express his thought, he grabs his wife and rushes out the door. It's a wise move.

I take off my glasses and rub my eyes in an attempt to regain composure, not noticing that a crowd of employees and several guests are silently arranged near the front desk, plainly waiting for my next move.

One of the recently arrived visitors among this unexpected audience leans over the counter and whispers to the manager. They alternately glance in my direction.

I brace myself as this conservatively dressed elderly gentlemen heads toward me. Reaching out with a reassuring hand, however, he says, "I don't know how you did it. Personally, I would've punched him in the nose if he spoke to me that way. You handled yourself quite well, under the circumstances."

An International Mood

Although the hotel staff invariably tolerates a degree of nonsense from guests in general, we have our limits. Working at the front desk requires you to smile even when a guest is screaming. In security, however, you're able to stop such behavior at a certain point, sometimes even stepping forward and over that line in response to belligerence.

It's around two-thirty in the morning. Sitting with a group of house officers in Harry's Bar after it closed, we spread out in a couple of booths while intermittently checking the lobby. There's zero activity in and around the hotel this particular night.

Suddenly a guest, I think he's Scandinavian, makes an abrupt appearance. He enters, shouting, "There's isn't a wet bar in my room!"

Sam, Vinny and I look at each other, our expressions revealing a similar thought pattern: here we go again.

"I've traveled all over the world," he continues, "and this is the first stinking hotel that did not have a wet-bar in my room."

Sam tells him he could order drinks from room service until four o'clock. Good idea. I figure Sven is relieved knowing now he could continue to drink, while leaving us free to consume our cheeseburgers in peace.

Instead, he whines, "I don't want to order from room service, damn it! I want a wet-bar in my room!"

"Some of the rooms do have wet-bars, sir," I interject. "Which one are you staying in?"

"I'm staying in room 817. What does it matter which room I'm in? There should be one in every room."

He's carrying on like a ten-year old girl who's lost her doll and won't settle for a replacement. Arguing with him is going to futile.

"The front-office manager would be glad to send your concerns to Mrs. Helmsley, sir. You'll find him at the other end of the lobby."

Sam and Vinny chuckle. Sven has no idea that I'm goofing on him.

"Give me a soda," he commands.

I point to an unopened bottle on the table next to him.

"Now have a good night," I say.

He deflects the hint.

"What about a glass? Surely you don't expect me to drink straight from the bottle as if I were some vagrant."

Vinny, who had just put a bottle of Coke to his lips, nearly chokes. Vinny wipes the Coke from his face, then gives the guest a glass. Unfortunately, it's not enough to make him go away. He just won't quit. To top it off, he starts bad-mouthing the United States. Another case of bad timing.

Earlier that evening I dealt with a foreign guest who endlessly spewed venom about how Americans are involved in only two things: "greed and thievery," as the Brit repeatedly put it. In that case, however, the anti-American visitor claimed that someone stole $500 from his room. I later discovered the Englishman had run up an unpaid tab at the bar equal to the amount of his alleged loss.

At this point I'm fed up. Not in much of an international mood, you could say.

Fortunately this clown gulps down his soda and leaves the bar before the situation gets out of control.

"I'm tired of assholes like that," Vinny says. "If we were in Finland, or wherever the hell he's from, they'd probably cut our tongues off for insulting their country."

"What can you do?" I respond. "These scumbags know we can lose our jobs if they report us for getting snotty with them."

"Then again," I continue, "he can't report us for something he doesn't see us do."

I hesitate before asking, "Didn't he say he was in 817?"

A mischievous smile appears on everyone's face.

Half an hour later, long after we assume the drunk is asleep, we step into the security office to, well, make a phone call. I retrieve a bullhorn from the closet, then call his room. He answers by the sixth ring. Having flipped the switch on the bullhorn to *siren*, I place the phone receiver inside the device and let a staccato *Whoop! -Whoop! -Whoop! -Whoop!* rip into the guest's ear.

Yeah, I know, it's not a nice thing to do. But under the circumstances it seems more than proper. Juvenile? Yes. But on the graveyard shift, successful efforts to break up the monotony are typically appreciated by all—not including Sven, of course.

We sprint back to the lobby and wait, but there's no response. No complaints from the manager. No sign of our favorite guest.

Time for round two.

This time, he picks up the phone by the first ring.

The siren cranked out another *Whoop! -Whoop! -Whoop! -Whoop!*

"Who is this?" he shouts into the receiver, nearly in tears. "What is going on?"

Whoop! -Whoop! -Whoop! -Whoop!

He slams down the phone, and we return to the lobby, fighting to preserve a poker face. A few minutes later the drunken guest emerges from the elevator, suitcases in hand. He marches past us without saying a word. Didn't even look at us, for that matter.

The soon-to-be-former guest passes the front desk and exits the hotel, managing to hail a cab immediately. We breath a collective sigh of relief. Our faces ache from laughter.

PART II
Fame

Ruined

Jean Claude Van Damme and an equally muscular, square-jawed male acquaintance appear in the hotel one evening, breezing through the Fiftieth Street entrance unnoticed. They head straight for the Towers, an intentionally isolated section of the hotel between the forty-first and fifty-fifth floors. With its own service desk and a set of elevators staffed 24 hours a day, it gives those who can afford it a level of privacy and comfort that average guests can only find in their dreams. Van Damme checks into a fifty-first floor, multiroom suite with a view of the cathedral. The pair enters the hotel and retreat to their room without any fanfare.

After walking to the other side of the main lobby, I slip into the newsstand to kill some time. Although Van Damme is now lounging in his posh quarters, I also discover that he's simultaneously standing in front of me—on the cover of Penthouse, that is.

Van Damme that month had become only the second such male ever to appear on the front of the men's magazine since boxer George Forman graced the cover a year earlier. No matter what one may think of Van Damme's acting abilities or the intellectual depth of his movies, he's a world-famous star, and an autographed copy of this edition of Penthouse was sure to be a collector's item. I wasn't about to let this future investment slip through my hands.

I buy a copy and sprint back to the Towers to see if the receptionist there has any pull in getting it signed. Indeed he does. In fact, having advance knowledge of the star's arrival, the clerk comes prepared with four 8 x 10 glossies of him. The photos are stored in a cardboard-backed manila envelope, ready for delivery. Van Damme, I learn, already has agreed to scribble his John Hancock on the photos.

"Could you? Please?" I ask the employee, Manny, as I hand him the magazine.

I didn't want to grovel, but this was, after all, a rare opportunity.

Manny shoves the porn rag under his personal mementos as well as a pile of Penthouses of which he has already been burdened by other employees.

"I guess I could," he says impatiently in an airy, timid tone.

He puts everyone's respective names on Post-it sticky notes and attaches them to each item, to distinguish them from his own memorabilia. The envelope with the 8 x 10s is prominently labeled with his name and workstation, with the words thickly inscribed in magic marker and stacked above one another: *Manny-Lykes-Tower-Desk.*

Manny rushes up to Jean Claude's luxury suite, giddy as a child. Soon after, his roommate returns our belongings. The name "Van Damme" stylistically emblazons the cover of my magazine, strategically written on the flexed arm gracing the cover.

Manny, however, isn't so pleased.

"What the hell is…I don't believe this!" he stammers with a shriek.

"What's wrong?" I ask.

He lies the photos on the counter to show me what has happened. Each is signed "Van Damme," but the actor was seemingly confused by the note on the envelope.

The scribbling on the first picture includes, *To Manny,* but the second is signed, *To Lykes,* the third *To Tower,* and the remaining photo, *To Desk.*

"I wanted to frame and hang them on my wall," Manny laments. "They're ruined."

"Waddaya kidding me? You couldn't ask for a better screw-up. A series of autographed photos with such a blunder? That's the equivalent of that famous postage stamp with the upside-down airplane. It *has to* increase the pictures' value."

"I'm not worried about their value," he says before walking away, nearly in tears. "They're ruined," he repeats.

I'm Pretty Sure I Ain't Mickey Mantle

The night manager and I are standing in the fortieth-floor suite of a confused—and drunken—guest. Cheryl and I listen as the admittedly drunk fifty-something man scratches his head, loosens his tie and jokingly expresses confusion about whether he's a Hall-of-Famer New York Yankee and has simply forgotten about this not-so-minor detail of his life.

"I've been out all day and maybe half the night," he says, "and I don't deny that I've had a bit to drink. But when I left this room today I did not have all this camera equipment and these baseball jerseys. I don't remember picking up the stuff. And I'm pretty sure that I ain't Mickey Mantle and never was, as far as I know."

He points to the jerseys on the bed and lets out a drunken cackle, an awkward, nervous laugh that halts with a discomforting snort. All the shirts have a '7" on the back of them, Mantle's retired number. In an adjacent bag are Mantle postcards and other memorabilia.

It's no mystery the items belong to the renowned Yankee slugger, whom I had seen just a few minutes earlier in the hotel's Hunt Bar with another Yankee legend, Billy Martin. After snooping around I learned that Mantle is registered in 4317, not 4817, to where a bellhop clearly in need of new glasses had accidentally delivered his belongings. Mantle and Martin are still in the bar as far as we know, but they had been there for some time. According to the employee serving them, they've been drinking straight Scotch whiskey for the past four hours. They're twice as drunk as the honest fellow who turns over Mantle's valuables, and therefore twice as volatile. We have to act fast.

"Someone forgot to tell them that they're supposed to sip Scotch, not gulp it," Tommy the bartender says.

A confrontation with them will be disastrous, as they might misinterpret our delivery of the goods to his room—half a day, that is, after he left them in the care of the bell captain—as an attempted theft of valuable collectors' items.

Mantle has been at the bar all night, from the moment he arrived at the hotel to drop off his bags. He leaves his stuff with a bellhop after playing in the annual Old-Timers' Game at Yankee Stadium and goes straight to the bar to meet Martin. Martin, as I vaguely recall, is boycotting the event over a lasting dispute with Yankees owner George Steinbrenner. This situation gives us the advantage we need, Not only is Mantle unaware his belongings had been in the hands of a stranger, to top it off he's extremely intoxicated. The location of his bags is, no doubt, the least of his worries. But like I said, bumping into him on the way to his room will result in a scene, maybe even a brawl, as his behavior over the decades would suggest.

As Mantle admitted in his memoir, *The Mick*, he and Martin had gotten so drunk in a hotel one night that they climbed out the window on to the ledge, and while hanging onto the sheer face of the hotel's outside wall they made their way partially around the building, peeking into other guests' windows to see what they were doing.

Right now, all we know is that the notorious duo is sitting on the edge of their bar stools, yapping. And fortunately, Mantle's wife is alone in her room when we get there. She's half-asleep and accepts the bags without any questions.

Mickey will never know that his stuff has been in limbo.

When we return downstairs we find Mantle and Martin saying good-bye before going their separate ways. Little do they know it's to be one of their last hurrahs, the end of a decades-long string of hell-raising and headline-creating drunken nights on the town.

Mantle wobbles toward the elevator, neither of us knowing that he's walking a few steps closer to his grave.

Though he'd outlive his old buddy by several years, Mantle nevertheless fares poorly in the end. He finally has the courage to seek treatment for his advancing battle with liquor, and publicly admits his baseball career would have been better and longer without that habit. But his liver already is too far-gone. Even a successful organ transplant isn't enough to save him. He passes away soon after the operation, although not from surgically related complications. Science helps him beat alcoholism, but can't rescue his soon-to-be cancer-riddled body from the Reaper.

Martin's then-fiancé greets him downstairs that night. He needs her support in traversing the lobby. They exit at Fifty-First Street. I then follow them outside from a safe distance. Martin's gross intoxication makes the pair easy targets for a predator, so I remain in view . Few street urchins pick out their victims when someone is standing nearby, watching over them with a portable radio in hand.

My efforts are a waste, since the biggest threat to their well-being is Billy Martin himself.

They cross the street and get into a burgundy Ford Fairmont convertible. I'm hoping they'll come to their senses and hail a cab. Martin insists that he drive, and unfortunately his partner relents. He's notoriously ill-tempered, especially when drinking booze. It's almost understandable why she doesn't demand the keys. This awareness of his infamous, rotten disposition while under the influence is exactly why I don't intervene. If he won't listen to his soon-to-be wife, there's little or no chance I can talk sense into him. He'll probably assault me if I try.

After starting the car, he throws it into gear, stomps on the accelerator and pulls into the path of speeding taxi. The cabby sees it coming and slams on his brakes, skidding to a stop within a yard of the driver's side door.

A few more feet and the taxi's front bumper would have been resting in Martin's rib cage.

Before the year is over, and under similar circumstances, his luck runs out. After a boozing it up in rural upstate New York, he gets into a car with another longtime acquaintance. Although it remains unclear who was behind the wheel that night (the "friend" initially took responsibility for driving, but later recanted), Martin's tumultuous life comes to an abrupt end, his crumpled body trapped in a vehicle at the bottom of a snowy embankment, on Christmas night, in fact.

No matter if he ignored the call of unseen forces of the universe, or if he simply failed to learn a lesson, a prelude to his demise had been silently noted at the Helmsley Palace.

Vacuum-Packed

From one moment to the next, separately I had witnessed the sudden appearance in the Palace of entertainers such as Liza Minelli, Faye Dunaway, Robert Mitchum, Charles Durning and Linda Evans. There were times when I found myself walking past characters including Elvira, Mr. T, or media husband-and-wife celebrities Maury Povich and Connie Chung. And as any fan of the Bronx Bombers surely would agree, it's not every day that you'd enter an elevator and unexpectedly see New York Yankee legend Phil Rizzuto standing there.

Also, what are the odds that you'll find the world's heavyweight boxing champion several feet from you, daring you to challenge him?

"Good evening Mr. Tyson. How are you, Mr. Tyson? Would you like a corner suite, Mr. Tyson? The bellhop will escort you to your room, Mr. Tyson. Enjoy your stay at the Helmsley Palace, Mr. Tyson. *Blah blah*, Mr. Tyson. *Bleeh blah-blah*, Mr. Tyson."

The new night manager is overdoing it just a bit. He's so zealous in accommodating Mike Tyson that we're thinking he going to drop to his knees and service him further, just for good measure. Tyson walks in the door moments earlier with two acquaintances, an unidentified white guy and a young black woman. Both tagalongs looked out of place. The nondescript white male just doesn't resemble a Tyson buddy or boxing cohort. Tall, lanky and a bit frumpy, the bespectacled young man is neither boxing-industry nor celebrity material. The girl is cute, but ordinary. Someone you picture with a working class guy like myself, not with an egotistical sports legend such as Iron Mike, who would soon hook up with the glamorous actress Robin Givens.

All employees near the front desk jump to attention, from the night manager to the bellhop. Like most unexpected appearances of famous characters, it's surreal to witness. But my colleagues checking the champ into his room have their noses so far up his ass that it made *me* feel uncomfortable.

Scott the elevator attendant and I stand off from the butt sniffing—far enough away that we don't feel obligated to join in, but close enough to witness our coworkers embarrassing themselves.

"I think I'm gonna puke," Scott says. "Just listen to this."

"Look at Tyson. He's just eating it all up," I say. "His head won't fit in the damn elevator if they keep it up."

Scott and I, and Hector from the cleaning crew, are the only other people in the lobby that are not attending to Tyson and friends. It's around three or four a.m. and the area is otherwise vacant. Once the front-desk folks stopped yapping all you can hear is the hum of Hector's vacuum, plugged in nearby. The bellhop escorts Tyson and the others toward the elevators. Despite the large gap between Scott and me and an adjacent wall, Iron Mike veers away from the open space and swaggers right toward us. He then walks between Scott and me, nearly bumping into us. I smirk out of a combination of annoyance and undeniable intimidation. Having caught me in the act of defying the current hotel status quo, his head jerks in my direction. Tyson stares me down, as if inviting a challenge to his invasion of our personal space.

For a split second, as he passes between us, I consider coughing in his face, pretending it's accidental. Not that I think he'll accept it as an accident. On the contrary, I'm sure he would have witnessed one accident that night, namely the "accident" I would have suffered from his bare hands. I momentarily accept this possibility, wondering if challenging his ego is worth a couple of jabs to my jaw and nose despite the resulting millions for which I could sue him.

Although nearly the same exact height and weight as Tyson, I'm under no illusion what will happen if so much as a breath or phlegm droplet travels from my mouth to his face: *I will feel pain.* And Tyson will experience joy, no matter how much cash he might later have to cough up.

Despite our wise unwillingness to stand up to the notorious professional bully, Scott and I win the final round. As Tyson tries to catch up with his minientourage, he makes the mistake of glaring back at me rather than paying attention to where he's going. As he looks over shoulder to stare me down some more, he trips over the cord from Hector's vacuum. He stumbles briefly, but catches himself.

"Awe, I'm sorry," Tyson says in his trademark high-pitched lisp.

We're not sure if his near fall is unintentional. Maybe he's simply playing it off smoothly, almost gentlemanly. Perhaps it's all an act, from the purposeful yanking of the cord to the insincere apology. Either way, he embarrasses himself, although we're sure he views himself as entertaining in the eyes of the obedient employees and his personal guests.

"What a dick-head," Scott says of his fellow Brooklynite, Tyson.

Hector comes over and plugs the vacuum cord back into the outlet. Meanwhile, Tyson approaches Hector, slipping him a twenty for inconveniencing the Dominican immigrant. Tyson then disappears into the elevator.

Turning to make sure Tyson was gone, Hector looks at the bill, slips it into his pocket and says to us, "Meester Tyson eez still—how do you say it?—he eez still an asshole."

Call it a Bonus

"We've got a problem," says Victor, the midnight security supervisor, outside the Arista Records annual Christmas gala. "Or should I say, Whitney Houston's manager has a problem."

We huddle around as Victor elaborates. After all, the record company is renting out two ballrooms on the fourth floor for the party. The place is teeming with celebrities and industry executives. In addition to stars of the eighties and nineties like Houston, Kenny G and Taylor Dayne, giants of the seventies such as Barry Manilow, Daryl Hall and John Oates, and Nick Ashford and Valerie Simpson also are present. No need to let on that all is not well at their merry event.

The security team steps away from the main hall's entrance. Victor whispers, "Houston's manager lost one of her bags."

"So?" I say with a shrug of the shoulders. "If we find it, we'll let her know."

Victor shakes his head and raises his hand as if instructing me to halt.

"This bag's got thousands upon thousands of dollars in cash and jewelry in it," he says. "Joey, you cover the ballroom door. Steve, follow the trail between here and the Tower Lobby. Frankie, you and I will split up and check the bathrooms, the fire stairwells, the entire freaking floor. Act casual. Don't walk around like you're looking for a lost wedding ring. Nonchalant, do you guys hear me?"

We launch our surreptitious canvassing of the area, careful not to spark the curiosity of onlookers. Most of the people at the party by now are drunk or were wired on cocaine. They're oblivious to everyone but themselves and their admirers.

As Frankie and I crossed paths moments later, he says, "May the best man win."

I stop in my tracks, puzzled at his comment.

"What's that supposed to mean?" I ask.

He rolls his eyes impatiently, continuing, "I don't know about you, but I could use that money more than that rich bitch can. Besides, I'm tired of putting up with these snotty bastards. Call it a bonus, if you want."

Houston, then in the early stages of her skyrocketing career, already has four number-one hits to her credit, as I recall. It's hard not to be at least a little envious of such success, but not enough to want to rob her. Maybe she'd never miss a bag full of jewel-studded necklaces and wads of cash. Then again, such a loss could bring the former church singer from Newark, New Jersey to tears. Who knows. What I did know is that Frankie and I were on a different wavelength when it came to possibly recovering Houston's valuables.

I'm admittedly so gung-ho that it never occurs to me to even consider keeping something that was lost and found. In fact, more than a few people call me a sucker for recovering, in an unrelated incident, a ruby necklace with stones so huge that anyone would assume they were fakes. But just as the Palace guests aren't your average hotel visitors, these rocks aren't ordinary jewels.

As I later learn from the general manager, the guest who left the ornamental neckpiece in her room was prepared to file a $35,000 insurance claim if the item didn't materialize.

My response to would-be thieves envious of the opportunity I passed up was, 'What the hell would I do with such a monstrous necklace?' No reputable jewelry dealer would touch such hot goods. What was my option, sell it some ghetto fence for a hundred bucks?

Fortunately for Houston's manager, in the end he embarrassingly realizes he never left his room without the bag of goodies. Can't tell if he's up to no good and simply changes his mind about the bag's "disappearance," or if he's just another flaky Hollywood type with his head so far up his ass that such an over-sight is normal. Didn't care at this point.

This bizarre yet welcome turn of events fits in perfectly with the skittish behavior of the other attendees. Arista's public relations flack approaches Mario and me and points out a couple who she claims are uninvited party-crashers, demanding they be ejected. We quietly surround the subjects, a guy in his fifties, wearing a tuxedo, smiling and dancing with a woman decked out in a flowing, blue gown, not much younger than he.

"All right, buddy, it's time to go," Mario says with his typical lack of diplomacy. "I'm the security supervisor and I'm informing you that this party is for invited guests only."

The couple stops dancing. They stare at Mario and me then burst out laughing.

"Who put you up to this?" the male asks with a smile.

"I bet it was Tommy. He's such a prankster," the woman says.

Mario, quickly becoming agitated, says, "Don't make me call the cops, sir, let's just…"

"What's going on?" another partygoer asks as he steps between Mario and the puzzled pair.

Mario starts to say, "Your coordinator over here told us...," then begins to turn toward the Arista flack who initially identified the couple as intruders. He cuts himself off, anxiously scanning the nearby crowd, realizing the accuser is nowhere to be found.

The intervener then identifies himself as one of Arista's vice presidents. Fortunately, he's gentlemanly about our mistake.

"Well, I don't know who told you they don't belong here, but I invited them personally," he says. "I suggest that next time you find yourself in such a situation, ask for a second opinion from someone. You're better off letting a couple of party-crashers off the hook than, well, embarrassing yourself as you just did."

Mario apologizes to the trio, who immediately resume dancing as if nothing happened.

The PR person re-appears, inquiring about the status of the trespassers.

"Your VP said they were with him," Mario says with a hint of annoyance. "What in the world made your think they didn't belong here?" he asks, pointing toward the falsely accused.

She stands there with her jaw hanging open, silent and seemingly confused.

"I didn't say *them*," she says angrily. "I was talking about those three over there."

She points at a different group this time, a twenty something male with two girls that couldn't have been older than nineteen.

"Are you sure this time? The last time you identified your boss' Mom and Pop, it seemed. Are your sure these three aren't his kids?" I ask, irritated that she put us in such an uncomfortable position.

"Yes, I'm sure. They're professional party crashers, in fact. They've been thrown out of other events. Get them out of here," she says as she starts walking away.

"Oh no you don't," Mario says, waving her over. "We'd appreciate it if you stayed nearby. Just in case."

Mario and I approach the young trio, trying to conceal our apprehension.

"Can we talk to you in the hallway?" he asks them collectively.

"What's this all about?" the male inquires. "Can't you see we're in the middle of dancing"

Once outside of the ballroom, Mario explains the situation to them.

"Just make it easy on yourselves and we won't call the cops."

One of the girls dramatically, and suddenly, expresses grief over her predicament.

"You have screwed up big time," she says, launching an accusatory diatribe. "You obviously have no idea who I am."

"You're right," I respond. "I have no idea who your are. Don't care either." I glance at people passing by and say, "Maybe someone else can vouch for you, okay Miss Popularity?"

One passerby takes a sudden interest, a slightly intoxicated man in his forties, staring curiously yet standing far away enough to remain uninvolved. That changes when I call for his participation.

"Excuse me sir," I say to him, erasing the grin from his reddened face. "I'm with house security and I'm trying to help these poor young people who apparently have lost their invitations. Are they with Arista Records?"

"Never seen them before," he says, quickly stumbling away.

I repeat the routine with a few other party-goers, all of whom shake their heads or look at the trespassers with a suspicious, squinty-eyed stare: negative, Charlie.

"Let's go people," I say, motioning the three over to the elevator. Their facial expressions try to hide the fact that they're *busted, exposed, embarrassed.* As we turn toward the opening compartment, a VIP entourage emerges, although this isn't immediately obvious to my People Magazine-reading self. The star status of a curvy, young lady at the front of this crew becomes obvious by the cheerleader-like reaction of, well, everyone in the vicinity, including the three clowns I now had in custody. The skimpy stage-production bodysuit painted on her body, plus the freaky mane of hair-extensions that drape down to the back of her rear-end, lead one to believe she's in show business—or perhaps spends way too much time in discotheques throughout the city's outer boroughs. I'm talking about somebody straight out of the Gum-Chewing, Tall-Haired Eighties Fashion Handbook, if you know what I mean.

The only difference is that she had, and created around her, an distinct, capitol-P *Presence.*

The crowd begins to descend slowly on the high-profile woman, who becomes smothered with compliments and congratulations from the row of Arista folks lining the hallway from the elevator to the ballroom doorway.

My detainees, being creative opportunists, try to ditch me as the spontaneously electrified herd closes in on the still-unidentified starlet.

"Don't even try it," I say. Mario and I then shove them, ever-so gently, of course, into an arriving elevator.

At this point we just want them out of the building. Although we usually process trespassers in the security office—take their picture, check their IDs and send them on their way—there's just too much activity in the building to warrant such an investment of time and energy. Once in the lobby, I tell them, "All right, now get your crusty asses out of here and don't come back. If you end up having such a lapse in judgment, you will no doubt find yourself in Manhattan Central Booking with all the other losers locked up by NYPD tonight.

The female, looking down several times at her skintight, sequined dress, as if all observers are expected to know what designer label was hanging on her butt, shouts, "Look at how I'm dressed! It's obvious I belong here. Do you realize who designed this outfit?"

Mario and I laugh in her face. Her performance makes for a great comedy routine if she wasn't so serious about trying to bully us. Although not easily intimidated, I allow her arrogant spiel to anger me. My hospitality-industry skills fly right out the window, you could say.

"I don't know, who did design your dress? Your pimp? Now get the fuck out of here before I kick you in your cheese-ball K-Mart gown," I say.

Everyone stands quietly, stunned by my remarks. Myself and Mario included.

"You've really done it now!" the girl screams as she storms toward the payphone. "I'm calling my uncle. He knows some important people in this city. You'll be unemployed before the night's over."

"And so will you if you don't get back to the Twelfth Avenue pier with all the other hustlers," I say.

Realizing that I stepped over the line with that comment, I knew it was time for these jokers to get out of the hotel. I took the phone out of her hand and slammed down the receiver.

"Out!" I commanded. "There's a payphone on Madison Avenue. Use that one. Now move!"

Finally, they left. But not before hurling obscenities at me and flipping a few middle fingers in my direction. For some reason, they were mad.

"You better chill out," Mario tells me. "You just can't talk to people that way, even if they deserve it."

He pauses before continuing, "Twelfth Avenue pier?…With other hustlers?…Did your pimp design that dress? Man, Peacock, you are a trip."

I'm not sure what had come over me. I mean, employment tends to be jeopardized when people, even trespassers, are spoken to like that. I otherwise knew not to cross that line. I guess sometimes you just get sick of people's nonsense. You make bad choices. Working weird hours will do that to a person.

The rage that I had hurled on this deceitful woman was unjustifiable. I think I just wanted to get back to the party, not stand in the lobby arguing with some kooky New Yorkers.

On my return to the ballroom, I wander anonymously among the celebrities and wannabes. Established musicians such as Herbie Hancock and George Benson pass by every few moments.

Suddenly, the music, and all dancing, stop in mid-song. Several spotlights and multicolored beams light up a small stage at the front of the room. Following a few rambling welcomes and holiday speeches from company executives, the music resumes playing. Specifically, I recall the song was "Tell It To My Heart," then a top-10 hit single by a singer from Long Island named Taylor Dayne.

Dayne, who as it turns out is the mystery woman everyone was giving red-carpet treatment to earlier in the party-crasher incident, gets up on stage and belts out her hit song. The intensity of her performance sweeps over the audience, as if she had lit a fire under everyone's feet. She ignites the inner dancer that apparently is itching to get out of each individual in attendance.

Next up was veteran Arista artist Barry Manilow. Despite the fact that he had a string of songs that topped the charts for decades, beginning when Dayne was still in diapers, Manilow's superstar status of the seventies and early eighties was a non-issue at the moment. He played a set so lifeless—Dayne's preceding performance notwithstanding—that the audience squeaked out a subdued round of applause seemingly out of pity more than respect.

Maybe he was feeling ill. Perhaps he simply had an off night. To Manilow's credit, however, he's still a household name in some circles, and continued to sell out concert halls into the new millennium. Taylor Dayne? To be sure, she had her moment in the sun, with two smash hits at the most. But try throwing her name around now, and people likely will say, 'Who?' or "Oh, yeah, I remember her.'

Staying power. Fifteen minutes of fame. Hmm.

As the event is winding down I slip away to the men's room. I approach an available wall-mounted urinal, a unit situated in the middle of three. Upon hearing a loud, almost exaggerated sniffing on my right, I can't help but to make a mental note of this disgusting, mucus movement. I don't dare glance over in response, which would have been an unwritten violation of men's room code. But upon the second phlegm inhalation, I look over with a sneer, like a second-grade teacher non-verbally communicating to a child to get a tissue rather than digest his throat-drippings.

I watch as he scoops a pile of white powder from a small, plastic bag, placing a makeshift, cardboard delivery device under his nose and snorting away, closing his eyes and wriggling his nose and upper lip around as if making sure every molecule of the drug was effectively absorbed into his nasal passage. The individual to my left is undertaking a similar task, only he's jamming a bullet-shaped metal device into his nose before snorting. In the stall behind me, more sniffing. Well, maybe that one had a cold. I couldn't see and didn't want to, for obvious reasons.

At the sink where I'm about to wash my hands, another cocaine cowboy is chopping lines on the counter top with a credit card.

"You want a hit?" the glassy eyed stranger asks.

"No, I'll pass."

"Are you sure? It's really good stuff. I mean, *primo* blow."

"I'll take your word for it."

It's time to exit candy land quickly. Wasn't my job to enforce drug laws. Especially when it came to high-profile guests, high on coke, no less.

Fortunately, my supervisor is nearby in the hall. Besides wanting to get away from the wired partygoers, for me the thrill of the event had dissipated. It was cool for a little while, but I had my fill.

"Hey, Mario. I'm gonna switch posts with Frank in the lobby, all right?

Mario nods, returning to yap with a guest who's looking to mingle with the so-called music elite rather than be pestered by some loathsome house dick.

I go downstairs and catch up with Frank, a recovering alcoholic who may have given up booze but had no chance of shaking his brash, stereotypical Brooklyn-Guido manner. In fact his Bensonhurst bravado emerges immediately on my arrival, just as pop-jazz artist Kenny G happens to walk by.

G, a rising Arista star who's celebrating his first platinum album, plays a flawless set at the party, including his smash instrumental single, "Songbird." As quickly as he appears on stage earlier that evening, he likewise goes from the crowd as soon as he's able. There's no sign of him until this moment. He wants to maintain a low profile.

Unfortunately for him, Frank picks him up on the celebrity radar screen, unable to sense that G wants to quietly return to his room without fanfare. Worse is the fact that G is holding a couple of identifiable bags of food from a well-known deli on Third Avenue. Perhaps the fourteen-dollar cheeseburgers from room service don't appeal to him, a wise choice, I might add, for reasons I don't care to elaborate at the moment.

G tries to slip into the elevator unnoticed. But my illustrious co-worker wants no part of that, figuratively shining a spotlight on him by shouting, "Hey, Kenny!

Brown-baggin' tonight, huh?" To top it off, Frank bursts into a loud, wheezing fir of laughter.

G, however, simply pulls a doughnut from his bag, looks us in the eye and takes a bite, smiling mischievously as the elevator doors closed.

Do You Know Who I Am?

"Security!" the service operator shouts over the radio. "Go to the front desk immediately!"

I rush across the expanse of the lobby, gradually slowing down as I get closer to the check-in area. The tone of the operator's voice signals that I've got little or no time for her to elaborate, despite what appears to be a crisis. So, I slow to a tip-toe pace. Peeking around a large, marble pillar to make sure someone isn't waving a gun, I'm prepared to run the other way, if necessary.

The only object being waved around is a room key. The docile clerk, standing alone with no obvious danger present, flinches as a he sees me, relieved at my appearance.

"Would you please hurry?" he says with a motherly cry. "Mr. Luther Vandross is locked out of his and he is quite upset."

"Luther Vandross?" I ask, aware the guest in question is a celebrity yet remaining ticked off that his VIP status is the only reason for the urgent nature of the "emergency" call.

"Yes, Luther Vandross," he responds "You do know who he is, don't you?"

"I'm well aware of whom Luther Vandross is, but…"

"Just please attend to him, immediately," the clerk says, cutting me off. "He is in, well, a rage, it seems."

Wonderful. It's after midnight. A high profile guest is stranded outside his room. Worse, this is happening because of the antiquated, cardboard key system that management refuses to replace, citing cost constraints. The hotel's leadership is averse to the notion of paying for 1,000 new locks. Not only that, but they'd have to replace the doors as well, since the old doors are custom cut to fit the old box-sized locks. I don't doubt that such a project would cost a fortune, but the Palace is losing customers because they're sick of being stranded outside their rooms every other time they attempt entry. The security chief can't grasp this fact.

There's no excuse to offer Vandross. Telling him the key system has flaws that need attending to won't cut it. Arriving at his floor, I prepare for the worst.

"Good evening, sir," I say, knowing there's nothing good to speak of, aware that evening has become morning. "Is there a problem."

The soul singer replies, "You're damn right there's a problem! This fucking key won't work!"

I stiffen up, eyebrows raised, looking at him as if he were crazy. You just don't speak down to another human being in that manner. Such condescension can get one hurt nowadays.

Then again, to him, I'm the peon, pauper guard-in-disguise, just another servant to whom orders are to be barked.

"Do you know I am?" he asks.

My body language conveys my annoyance to him as I lower the key away from the door and stare ahead of me. He's about to set the record straight, I guess. I lose track of where he's taking this predicament, having taken a closer look at his attire.

Although acting as if he were the Palace Prince, his garb didn't fit the title. His baby-blue cotton pajamas reminded me of what I was wearing in Christmas pictures from the early 70s, when as a child, freshly awoken and excited Santa had come, I pose with my new presents under the holiday tree.

I ignore his question. The abuse mounts.

"I could've been mugged in this fucking hallway waiting for you," he says. "What the hell took you so long?"

Quieting him down would've been simple—if I only had a pocket-sized camera with me. The gossip magazines would've launched a bidding war for such photos. Imagine, a photo of Luther Vandross standing in his pajamas in a hotel hallway, whining like a baby instead of singing proclamations of love. Those pix wouldn't have pulled in a set-for-life pile of cash, but the payout would've tided me over while I searched for a new job.

I reprogram his lock with an electronic gizmo I've brought back from the security office, specially designed as a short-term solution to this chronic lock-failure problem. I hand back his key, not bothering with the standard apologetic speech I usually give to guests under such circumstances.

My silence heightens his agitation.

"Have you nothing to say?" he asks.

A wisecrack about his current state of fashion seems fitting. Similar to the time I almost coughed in boxer Mike Tyson's face as he invaded my personal space, the temptation to provoke Vandross to aggression is alluring. One swing from him and "KA-CHING," wait for the cash register to slide open.

He storms into his room, then just as quickly he backtracks, pointing in my face and shouting, "Never again will I stay in this hotel! Never!"

Vandross slams the door behind him and begins trashing the room. Dishes breaking, tables flipping, the whole temper-tantrum thing. Like a 5-year-old who's locked out his toy box for a while and is then allowed to play. Chaos.

"Never again! Never again!" The wailing resounds down the corridor, following me into the elevator like a bad odor.

The incident takes place before what I regard as my recovering-Neanderthal days, a period of awakening which will elude me for years to come. In other words, rather than taking the higher path of walking away and forgetting, my face becomes flush with anger, so resentful am I that I had restrained myself from slamming a fist into his mouth in mid-whine. He would have deserved it, some might argue. But his behavior didn't earn the right to a cash settlement from the Helmsleys if I had broken his jaw, a remedy necessary to quash a potential front-page, headline-grabber about the continuing troubles of the Helmsley hotel empire. I wasn't about to make Luther Vandross richer, nor myself poorer.

Signature Surveillance

A denim-clad, fortyish woman wearing dark shades poises herself by the lobby elevators, across from several rows of luggage that gradually sprouted next to the grand staircase. Bellhop after bellhop lines up additional bags as each moment passes. At the opposite side of the corridor, I situate myself by the growing array of suitcases. I scan the guests' valuables in addition to every person that came near. So does the sneaky looking female, but for different reasons, I surmise.

Can't fool me with those sunglasses, lady. I see you scoping out the situation. It's seven in the morning in the middle of winter. It's still dark, in case you haven't noticed. I see you eyeing those bags. Looking for opportunity? Yeah, so am I: the opportunity to apprehend your thieving ass and have you hauled off to jail.

Management is temporarily using the waiting area to accommodate a sudden rush of checkouts. So many guests are exiting the hotel that morning that they fill the bell captain's storage room to capacity, requiring the attendants to use alternate means of securing the luggage. The guests pay their bills at the cashier's desk, confident that their stuff is secure.

The arrangement is a bag-booster's dream, the set-up where an enterprising felon could walk away with his or her pick of rich travelers' goods. Although the average luggage-pilferer is a well-dressed professional, not adorned with shabby clothes and stringy hair, as was my current subject's condition, I continue to watch. Glancing around, she's noticeably tense. She warrants further surveillance.

"Freddie, meet my downstairs," I call to a colleague on my portable radio. "I think I might have something."

We meet behind one of the massive, bogus marble pillars next to the main staircase, out of the suspect's view.

"What's up?" Freddie asks.

"There's a woman over by the elevators—don't look yet, she just looked this way—who's either been eyeing me or that stack of bags," I said. "I think she's up to no good. Might be looking for a freebie, if you ask me."

"Are you sure her bags are not over there?"

"Nah, man, are you kidding me? Take a look at her. She looks like she just crawled in from the street."

Freddie then positions himself on the mezzanine, above the luggage, out of the suspect's view. He looks down at me and nods, recognizing that our subject is worthy of close observation. A sudden scream echoes across the ornate waiting area. Freddie shrugs his shoulders, lifting his hands in front of him, palms up, as if waiting for a signal from me to sprint down the stairs. I shook my head, uncertain where or whether a crime is in progress.

The teenage clerk from the lobby newsstand hands the suspect a pen and pad. Our target, clearly irritated by the encounter, quickly scribbles an autograph and handed it to the excitable young woman.

Baffled at what took place, I intercept the youngster as she heads back to the newsstand. An autograph? Must be a case of mistaken identity.

"Excuse me, miss," I say hesitantly, "but why in the world did you ask that woman for her autograph?"

"What do you mean, 'why'? That's Bo Derek! I can't believe I just got her autograph!"

"I can't believe it either."

"What do you mean?"

"Um, never mind."

I'm not about to elaborate.

Freddie then approaches me, grinning. He cracks a sly grin, squinting curiously, expecting an explanation.

"Would you mind telling me what the heck is going on here?" he asks.

"Well, let's just say I was wrong about our suspect," I say. "She's definitely not what—or who—I thought she might be."

He stares intently, waiting, certain there's more to come. He's also aware that our subject had jotted something down for the girl. It's obvious there's more to the situation than I'm letting on to, Freddie's expression hints.

"All right, all right," I say. "It wasn't a bag-booster. It was…"

I can't say it. Although my error is forgivable, even harmless, it's a gross misjudgement. It pains me to reveal this.

"You were saying?" Freddie prods.

"It was Bo Derek."

He stares silently.

"As in Bo Derek, the actress?" I say as well as ask, thinking he doesn't recognize the name. "Bo Derek, you know, the one from the movie '10'?"

A delayed chortle erupts from within him. He nearly chokes as he cackles.

Regaining composure, he pats me on the back and said, "Keep up the good work, kid."

Just then, Bo's husband John Derek exits an elevator and takes her by the hand, escorting Bo to an awaiting limo.

And Your Little Dog, Too

Despite the recognizable faces and voices of the stars, it's easy to overlook a celebrity standing right in front of me. When you go to a movie or turn on the tube or the radio, you eagerly expect celebrity characteristics to spill into your eyes and ears. But most people never get closer to famous figures than a close-up head-shot on TV. Screen stars always look taller, fatter, shorter or skinnier than they appear on screen. As a result, I have several other surprise encounters—and a few close calls that crept toward the edge of disaster. Luckily for me these incidents are with some of the more good-natured folks from the entertainment world.

Around the time that Leona Helmsley is being separately tried by the State of New York and the federal government for tax evasion and other alleged crimes, I switch from the graveyard shift to the day tour. Although the return to daytime hours restores a sense of normalcy to my sleep pattern, the bizarre state of affairs at the Palace stemming from Leona's highly publicized trial keeps all else in my work-life in near-disarray. The worse business gets, the less compensation and perks make their way to the employees. And as more and more workers either lose their jobs or watch their tip-dependent wages evaporate, the less inclined they are to kiss the buttocks of the dwindling number of visitors. Hence, fewer paying guests.

New York's then-only Five Diamond hotel was on a rapid, downward slide.

Making matters worse one particular afternoon is a report that the jury in Leona's trial is about to reach a verdict. The uncertainty of the outcome is affecting her already inconsistent management style. And it affects the rest of us, too, since no one knows what to expect of Leona from one day to the next. Silent? Screaming? Sober? Drunk? One can't predict such a thing.

A doorman from the Park Lane Hotel, Leona's residence on Central Park South, tips us off that the boss is on her way to the Palace for lunch. Employees at Helmsley properties across Manhattan make such a courtesy call when Leona is en route from one location to another.

The TV movie "Queen of Mean," based on the book by journalist Ransdell Pierson, captured that unwritten company procedure. Pierson had done his homework well, for I can attest to how accurately the movie and book documented the employees' joint efforts; just like the real thing, they showed how we made a call to the other building's security team or door staff and anonymously uttered, "Mama's on her way," or, "The eagle has flown." Also, upon Leona's arrival, these cryptic phrases were repeated by radio, phone, word-of mouth, however possible and by whomever available. Once transmitted from building to building, buzz of the Queen's imminent arrival ricocheted from the lobby out-ward, spreading like a spider's Web to every corner wherever employees were present, from the basement to the roof.

Upon receiving the alert that day, all employees stand like wooden soldiers in anticipation. Planting oneself like a fixture gives you a fifty-fifty shot of avoiding Leona's scrutiny; either she views you as a dedicated servant prepared to take care of her darling guests, or she accosts you with hostile accusations that you're loaf-ing and aren't worthy of being employed under the beneficent umbrella of the Helmsley Empire.

It depended on which way the wind was blowing on a given day. For instance, Leona fired a front desk manager because she found cigarette butts in the lobby. True, the cancer sticks were extinguished in a hotel-supplied ashtray, within the artificial boundaries of a section designated for smoking, but that mattered little to Leona.

The effects of that unwarranted firing are long-lasting, too. For as long after the incident as I can remember, lobby attendants and mid-level managers alike regularly yank cigarette butts out of the trays, sometimes before the embers stop glowing. That's how afraid the staffers were that their heads might be next in line, lopped off for the crime of ignoring dirty ashtrays.

Additionally, Leona once terminated, then later rehired, her main chef—beads of water were visible on the lettuce in her salad, and she had become so enraged that she had him escorted out of the building during prime lunch hour.

In light of these outlandish spectacles by Mrs. Helmsley, I almost lunge at a petite, well-dressed older woman who enters the lobby one day with a micro-scopic dog at her side. Having received the ever-reliable *Eagle Has Flown* message moments earlier, I rush her to get back outside, anxious to expel the animal lover before Leona sets eyes on her.

"Excuse me, ma'am," I say while motioning toward the exit. "I can't allow you to bring that dog in here. You'll have to leave. *Now*, please. Thank you."

"But I have an appointment at the hair salon," she retorts calmly.

Glancing outside, hopeful that Leona's stuck in traffic somewhere and isn't about to pull up to the curb in her limo, I look down at the cute, sniffling pup, and say to the woman, "I'm sorry, you'll have to take him outside," followed by an urgent yet diplomatic, "Please."

Leona would've lost her mind if she had seen me talking to someone with a dog in the lobby. No excuse would have sufficed.

The still-unidentified lady playfully responds, "All right, I'll leave. I'll just tie the poor dog to a pole or something."

She exits without complaint. Two bellhops immediately descend upon me.

"I can't believe you just threw out Joan Rivers," one of them says.

"She is such a nice lady, too," adds the other.

We all stand there silently, uncomfortably. Well, at least *I'm* standing there uncomfortably. I begin to speak, then pause briefly, wondering if they're joking.

"That was Joan Rivers?" I say. "Are you kidding me, or what?"

They shake their head in unison. It's no joke.

I rush outside to apologize for my haste. Luckily, my inability to recognize her isn't an issue.

"Um, excuse me. Mrs. Rivers?" I say, interrupting a conversation she's having with one of the doormen. "I'm sorry I asked you to leave so abruptly, it's just that Mrs. Helmsley is on her way and, well, I guess I panicked. I don't want to give her an excuse to say something to me."

Rivers hesitates, looks at the doorman, then back to me. Her hesitancy is intentional, just to make me sweat.

She finally breaks the ice and says, "No problem. If I were you, I wouldn't want to talk with her either."

Despite wanting to accommodate her, I don't want to leave myself vulnerable to Leona's wrath. I offer to meet Rivers halfway.

"I have an idea," I say. "Would you mind holding the dog as you walk through the lobby? Would that be okay?"

I feel like a schmuck for bothering her, but I didn't have much choice. Considering that Mrs. Helmsley had once turned down Michael Jackson's request to rent a room for his pet monkey, it was unlikely she'd be receptive to a having a rat-sized dog traipsing across the lobby rug.

Rivers picks up her dog and informs him, "This will only take a minute, Spike." She reenters the building, and not a moment too soon. The Helmsleys arrive minutes later.

As it turns out, Leona didn't say a peep to anyone. That would have been different if Spike had been hovering around her ankles, however.

About fifteen minutes later I sense someone tapping on my shoulder from behind. It's Rivers, with Spike partially concealed in her jacket. As if passing off state secrets to a foreign agent, she positions herself next to me, slowly glancing from side to side, and whispers, "I'm coming back at three o'clock. I'm gonna put a disguise on the dog before I do You'll never recognize him."

No doubt it was in everyone's best interest that Leona and Rivers didn't cross paths, considering Helmsley's volatile state of mind. Who knows Maybe if an exchange indeed took place, it would have been limited to a brief, yet cordial (and transparently phony) salutation by the Queen of the Palace. Then again, it could've erupted into a confrontation a la MTV's Celebrity Death Match, the play-by-play fictitious claymation spectacle of famous characters humorously tearing each other limbs off. (In fact, Leona in one episode of CDM had been paired off with former Philippine First Lady Imelda Marcos, whom I believe at one point jammed a high-heeled shoe into Helmsley's temple.)

Anyhow, imagine this: the Helmsleys get to the hotel a few minutes earlier than they actually did that day, and Leona sees Rivers entering the hotel with little Spike trailing behind. Leona stops her, commencing an interrogation that would make a 1960s parochial school teacher proud.

"And where do you think you are going with that filthy animal?" Helmsley might ask. "Who gave you permission to bring that mutt into my Palace?"

Rivers then would take the verbal assault in stride, saying, "Yeah, sure lady. Have another Scotch and soda. You'll be fine. Really."

"Who do you think you're talking to?" Leona might respond with Brooklynite gruffness and redundance. "Who do you think you're talking to?"

Rivers would say, "A scarecrow with a lousy makeup job, maybe?"

Such a battle could be bottled and marketed. If only boxing promoter Don King were around that week.

The Living Dread

Shouting suddenly emanates from the elevators, followed by the sound and sensation of someone running toward me. I'm parked on that couch for hours, mind you, unable to detach myself after sinking ever-so-slightly into its plush material. Thinking something traumatic is taking place, I jump up defensively.

The boisterous man responsible for disrupting my nap stops running and launches into a set of jumping jacks.

"Come on you people, look alive!" exercise guru Richard Simmons commands. "Don't just sit there, get that blood flowing!"

He bounces around the lobby, exhorting the masses to get pumped up, much to the dismay of his target audience. The sleep-eyed guests just stare silently. I do likewise. Don't think for a second it might be necessary to dissuade Simmons from making a commotion. It's not every day such an illustrious figure passes, and definitely not in this manner.

Like a ballerina on methamphetamine, Simmons prances across the lobby to 51st Street, where a black stretch limo awaits him. Despite only wearing a pair of shorts and a tank top, he embraces the frigid winter air with delight, filling his lungs and exhaling a frosty cloud that swirled around his head.

Unaware of his destination, I go home soon after, tuning into the Howard Stern Show on the radio. Simmons happens to be the featured guest of the live program. He describes a scenario in which the living dead are all around him. This unnamed place of beauty has the greatest view in all of New York City, but is infiltrated by lifeless human beings, both young and old, he says.

"You should have seen some of these people, Howard," he says. "Sitting on the couch and staring at the floor as if they dreaded living. Tragic."

The still-secret location he's rambling about is the Palace. Instead of simply observing Simmons in the lobby, I've become the observed. My anonymous, lethargic presence is the highlight of a globally recognized fitness fanatic's discussion on nationwide syndicated radio. Out of millions of people tuning into Stern, I may have been the only one—*hopefully* the only one—intimately aware of what inspired Simmons' lamentations.

PART III
Thieves

Nice Accent, Tommy

Opportunity. Some crooks seize it, often stumble across such chance circumstances to commit crime. At the Palace, however, most thieves actively seek opportunity, or more succinctly, create opportunity. Those who employ stealth and deception are most successful.

Surprisingly, most guests act as if an impenetrable shield surrounds the building, blocking out such bad guys. Instead of placing jewels in safe-deposit boxes available at the main cashier, some guests leave the items exposed on a table in their room, only to "disappear" while they're out. Similarly, despite the availability of a storeroom behind the bell captain's desk, they drop off their luggage unattended in a remote corner of the lobby, probably to forgo leaving a tip, as they sit in the restaurant for an hour having breakfast.

What could possibly happen to us? some must think. We're in the Helmsley Palace!

Reality sets in when they find out their two-thousand dollar Louis Vuitton luggage set mysteriously walked away.

While far from being crime-ridden, the Palace is a great target for an ambitious crook. If a criminal has the guts or skill to do a job with a potentially big pay-out, they logically select a Helmsley hotel over a Marriott, just as they'll choose to steal a Rolex instead of a Timex if given the choice.

Adding to the vulnerability of the guests is their naivete about crime. Judging by their actions, seemingly they assumed the interior of the hotel was a safe haven from the criminal element, no different from the pampered confines of their offices and chauffeured cars.

Well, that isn't the case.

Most, but not all, perpetrators must view overt aggression as unnecessary. After all, why use or threaten to use force when you can walk away with another person's property undetected?

If you get caught carrying out a larceny, you might face days or weeks in jail, maybe a few months at best, followed by a fines or community service if you bothered showing up for their court appearances. But those same valuables, if taken by force, hypothetically can land you in the state penitentiary for several years.

Call it a street-level form of risk-analysis, taken to the extreme.

It's a rarity that these perps leverage violence in and around the hotel to commit crime. In fact, these particular cases are so unusual that at first I doubt they take place.

A group of men are partying late one evening in Harry's Bar. One of them leaves to use the rest room on the mezzanine. Moments after he drops his pants and sits on the toilet an arm appears from outside the stall. This person, whom the victim mistakenly guesses is a friend playing a practical joke, points a gun at him while hiding his face.

"Give me your pants," the robber says, "and don't try taking out the wallet."

"That's real funny Tommy. What kind of accent are trying to imitate anyhow?"

The accent turns out to be real. So does the gun.

"Give me the pants or I'll blow your head off!"

The robber then cocks the trigger. Hmm. Must not be Tommy after all.

The victim takes off his shoes and kicks the pants towards his assailant.

"Wait ten minutes before you get up, 'cause there's somebody waiting outside that'll kill you if you come out any sooner," the thief warns.

Rightly or wrongly, the victim complies with this command, waiting fifteen minutes or more before peeking outside and asking for help. We call the police and the pant-less visitor agrees to give a statement, confirming the act had occurred. Unable to get description of the Bathroom Bandit, other than the color of his sleeve and the kind of gun he used, N.Y.P.D relegates the case to its archives, filed with thousands of other unsolved crimes for the statistical year.

It Was So Romantic

"Security, the guest requests immediate assistance in room 1401."

"Ten-four, operator."

Here we go again, I say to myself aloud. One never knows what a guest wants when they're demanding immediate attention from security. A loss report they want to file? Maybe they just need someone to talk to since their psychiatrist is unavailable.

Once I had responded to an "immediate attention" call only to find some wacky Englishman complaining that his "balls felt tingly." It was impossible to predict what might happen next.

The guest in 1401 opens the door. He's holding a bloodstained washcloth to his nose.

"Please come in," he says like a woman in distress.

I enter the room at a leisurely pace, looking around for anything that could jeopardize my safety. All seems in order, with the exception of the bloody nose. Two half-eaten meals sit on a room-service cart near the bed.

"What happened?"

The guest begins to sob, telling me the sequence of events that led to his bloody nose. His mannerisms are effeminate to the extreme, almost exaggerated, as if performed during a Steve Martin skit. I find it difficult to maintain my composure. His behavior is like a parody of someone else, peppered with a hard-to-believe lisp, no less.

"I met Shawn," he tells me, "in a club not too far from here. We hit it off so well that I invited him to my room for, you know, a late-night dinner."

Seeing that this is turning into a drawn-out story, I ask him to get to the point.

"Well, the food arrived and we began to eat," he says. Rolling his eyes to dramatize what had been a dreamlike-state of mind, he continues, "It was so romantic."

He pauses, then switches emotional gears. Between sobs he squeaks out, "And then suddenly, out of nowhere, Shawn leaned over the table. I thought he was going to kiss me, so I closed my eyes and waited."

Then he lowers his eyelids and puckers his lips slightly, as if reliving the anticipation before an imminent, passionate kiss.

Angrily, he continues, "And that's when the son of a bitch hit me in the face. He knocked me down and took all of my money. Then he ran out the door."

No one deserves to be assaulted or to have their belongings taken from them. But when I hear about people in situations in where they leave themselves so vulnerable to strangers, I'm compelled to ask, "What do you expect?"

It's not that I'm insensitive to victims of crime. It's just baffling to me that people ignore the inherent danger of certain predicaments. I don't know if it's a curse or a blessing that I'm hyper-aware of such hazards, but I'd rather look over my shoulder now instead of mug shots of convicted felons later.

Take a Walk on the Wild Side

After arriving in the city earlier than usual one night, I head to a deli on Third Avenue for a cup of coffee. It's about an hour before midnight. On the East Fifty-First Street side of a Park Avenue office building, a group of people congregate in an open public space along its perimeter, engaging in a combination of conversation and non-verbal communication via hand gestures.

In some cities this scene might catch your attention, in light of the hour of night and the absence of residential buildings in the vicinity. But in New York, the end of the three-to-eleven shift seamlessly melds into the beginning of the graveyard tour, like an endless stream of relay runners passing the baton from one player to the next. Each shift change, day or night, is like a continuance of a race, with varying degrees of traffic on the track.

A short and stocky middle-aged man, a blue-collar worker of some sort, walks past the public space in question. Being parallel to him on the other side of the street, I detect two people from the above mentioned group breaking away from the rest of their crew. The pair walks down the steps to street level. They surprise the man from behind.

Must be friends of his trying to scare him. No reason to think otherwise, considering they were smiling as they approached him.

One yanks his wallet out of the man's back pocket, however, as the other strips the watch from his wrist. The smaller perp repeatedly punches the victim in the chest, or so I thought. A nearby female passerby stumbles upon the scene. She screams. I sprint to the police station one block away.

On returning to the hotel, I tell the security supervisor, who happens to be a retired New York City cop, that I witnessed a robbery.

He asks, "Well, what did you do?"

"I went to the precinct and reported it," I say. Such citizen involvement is the right thing to do, of course, I'm thinking. I also assume that in some way my actions will put me on good terms with my new boss.

"You did what?" he screams. "You didn't leave your name, did you?"

"Of course I left my name," I respond, puzzled. "I told them to call me here if they needed me."

He throws his hands in the air, exasperated.

"And what if they call you? Then I gotta pay someone overtime to cover for you! I can't believe this."

The phone rings. It's an NYPD detective. Says he'll send a patrol car to pick me up. Wants me to give statement.

Before hanging up he asks, "By the way, which one had the knife, the short one or the tall one?"

"The knife?"

"Yeah, the knife. You did witness the robbery, didn't you?"

"They were stabbing him? Holy smoke, I thought they were punching him!"

"Nope. He's got numerous holes in his chest." He pauses before continuing, "This could end up a homicide."

I nearly drop the phone. Didn't know what to say.

The detective continues, "Anyhow, I'll see you in a bit."

A terrible guilt sweeps over me. If I had only picked up a brick or something from a nearby construction site. If I had thrown something at them, anything, maybe the victim wouldn't have gotten so badly injured.

The guilt fades later when I find out there were other witnesses, but none willing to get involved. Even the screaming woman, the one on the same side of the street on which the robbery took place, refuses to give a formal statement.

If the victim dies, I'm the sole witness.

Uncooperative witnesses aren't the only problem. First, the victim says he was robbed by a man and a woman. However, I say it was two men, one with long hair like a woman. Second, the suspects that the cops apprehend are Mexican. Since it was dark, I can't say for sure what race they are. And when I go to the Midtown North precinct to give a written statement about my observations, a patrolman accidentally walks the suspects into my room. As a result of this procedural error, the police don't ask me to pick them out of a lineup.

Why bother. Such an arrangement was a defense attorney's dream come true.

The victim eventually recovered from his wounds. But I never testify in court for his sake. The District Attorney's Office has no choice but to plea bargain with the suspects . There are simply too many holes in the case, no pun intended.

About two hours after the incident, I wander around the lobby as if the fog has rolled in. I'm emotionally spent. A Hasidic man approaches me and asks, "Is it safe in this area? My wife and I want to take a walk."

Before witnessing this violent act, I would have gladly (and honestly) told them the area was relatively safe, even at night. But with the robbery fresh in my mind, however, I didn't know what to tell them.

Informing the guests about an attempted murder so close to the hotel isn't a good move from a business perspective. Yet, withholding the truth is tantamount to sending them into a jungle blindfolded.

"It shouldn't be a problem," I tell them, while at the same time pointing in the opposite direction of the stabbing incident, and say, "but I strongly recommend you walk towards Fifth Avenue. There are more cops patrolling that area."

They glance at one another without turning their heads, then cast their gaze back at me. The husband shakes his head and without hesitation escorts his wife to the elevator. A romantic walk through Rockefeller Center is out of the question.

Nine Seconds To Get Away

A doorman is unloading a guest's belongings from the trunk of a limo onto a luggage-cart at the curb, just a few feet away. He takes one item from the vehicle, places it on the cart, picks up another item, and so on. He removes about ten items from the car as the guests wait in the lobby. By time the employee wheels the cart to the front desk, only nine pieces are left.

The guests-victims are a well-known, married couple and an executive team for a major tobacco producer. In light of the level of power they held at Coffin Nails, Inc., rumors spread among the Palace employees that the theft involves corporate espionage. Perhaps it does. Then again, such speculation is grounded in pure fantasy. No one knew for certain.

But no matter if the culprit or culprits had been scoping out the routine of the doorman or if they just happened to be walking by and acted spontaneously, it was opportunity, not conspiracy, that led to this crime.

Another incident I encounter, although not as dramatic, exemplifies the limited amount of time it takes to execute the simplest of larcenies.

A woman one morning claims that someone had stolen her purse from the lobby couch. She's baffled such a thing could happen "at a place like the Palace." Less distraught over her loss than about where the loss occurred, she demands an explanation.

"Before I try to explain," I say, "would you mind telling me where you were when the theft took place?"

"I was sitting on this couch when I realized I had to make a quick phone call."

"And you left the purse on the couch?"

"Yes."

"Unattended?"

"I don't know what you are insinuating," she responds, "but I was gone for maybe ten seconds."

"Well, ma'am, forgive me saying so, but you gave them nine seconds to get away. Do you know what I mean?"

Unwilling to acknowledge an indirect contribution to her loss, she storms out of the hotel before I can file a report or call the cops.

Professional thieves, not street thugs, often are the perpetrators of such crimes, evidenced by the fact that victimized Palace guests rarely can pinpoint when their respective losses take place. More often than not the hands on the clock are in an altogether different position by time they discover something is missing, a sure sign a pro is involved.

The pros' main asset is stealth. Even with a couple of plainclothes house officers and a couple of surveillance cameras in the lobby it's difficult to detect a pro at work. On a busy day dozens of guests simultaneously check in and check out. It's impossible for security to distinguish one man in a suit from another, while also matching every bag and briefcase with their owners.

Opportunity abounds for a professional bag-booster to slip in and out of a crowd undetected. If a well-dressed white male (or of any other race) puts down a briefcase and walks away, and then a few minutes later another well-dressed man of the same ethnicity picks up that briefcase, it's difficult to discern whether it's the same person who put it there in the first place.

The victims' lack of awareness, combined with the snakelike boldness of the perps, provides an advantage over even an unusually alert guest or even an experienced house officer.

"Excuse me, sir. You have mustard on your jacket," someone might say to the oblivious world traveler.

The guest turns around to see what's on him, and verifies that he does indeed have mustard on his brand new suit.

"Let me get that for you," the stranger insists, "I have a napkin right here."

He obliges, and allows the polite fellow to assist.

"Well, I got most of it off, but it looks like you're going to need to have it dry cleaned."

"Thank you," the guest says, "I appreciate it."

His appreciation is sincere, until he realizes he's been duped. While the "polite" stranger wipes the mustard away, a partner walks away with the guest's briefcase. By time the guest realizes it, both crooks already were heading for their next job.

I don't claim to know every scam and deception on earth, although experience has blessed me with keen eyes and ears to pick up on such fraud. No one, however, can possibly know every trick and their myriad variations. I learn this the hard way when a couple of ghosts pulled off a scam practically under my nose.

Turning Japanese

A group of Japanese businessmen stand in a semi-circle in the lobby, paying homage to their boss. For me, it's a free cultural lesson. The lowest in the corporate hierarchy bow their heads at a ninety-degree angle. The middlemen lean forward just a little. Nodding his head ever so slightly is the chief.

About ten minutes later I find out I'm not the only one taking note of this display of power and submission.

One of the Japanese gentleman approaches me, struggling through his thick accent and basic grasp of English that one of their briefcases was missing. He leads me to a row of about twenty bags that were neatly lined against the wall. He points to a cavity in the row where the missing item allegedly once was.

"Are you sure you had put it there?" I ask.

He shifts from side to side, scratches his head and says with a nervous laugh, "Oh, I am quite sure. I am the assistant to the president of our company. I had placed his bag there myself."

His face exudes worry, like a first-time patient waiting in the examination chair for his new dentist. It's an unmistakable look, silently signaling he definitely placed the briefcase where he had claimed.

I ask if anyone approached the group, figuring that someone squirted one of them with mustard or some other liquid as a distraction.

No one had gotten squirted, but someone indeed diverted their attention.

While they stood around in that semi-circle arrangement, a suit-and-tie kind of white dude walks up to them, points to a dollar bill on the floor and asks, "Did someone drop that money?" The prospect of losing money being an important issue, all turn to look. All faced away from their briefcases at this point. More than likely, as they were checking their pockets and staring at the bill on the floor, a partner of the "well-dressed American," as they described him, had picked up the briefcase and walked away.

Not just any briefcase, but the briefcase belonging to the top man of the group, the president of one of the largest automobile manufacturers in the world.

All of this occurs, unknown to me, fewer than twenty feet away from where I'm standing. The assistant questions me on this matter as his associates stood nearby, waiting for me to speak.

"Were you not standing right over there?" he asks.

"Well, I was, but I had been walking around as well."

They look at one another and immediately begin a rapid-fire conversation in their native tongue. My response clearly isn't to their liking, understandably; because there's allegedly ten thousand dollars worth of cash and travelers checks in that briefcase.

The theft and my inability to detect the crime doesn't exactly boost the image of my department. At least a videotape isn't available of me being figuratively blind-sided. Another house officer in a similar predicament isn't so fortunate.

"You have to see this tape," one of the guys from the four-to-twelve shift tells me as I arrive for work. Popping in the video, I see it's a surveillance tape of the front desk and its surroundings. Standing in front of a loaded-down luggage rack is a new officer, a retired cop I'll call Sam. With his back against the rack he glances around from left to right, trying to look attentive. His illusion of attentiveness is ineffective. A bag-booster nonchalantly picks up a briefcase—which was resting on the same rack Sam thinks that he's guarding—and strolls out the door.

Sam keeps looking from side to side—a few seconds to the left; a few seconds to the right; stare straight ahead; back to the left, and so on—like a programmable figurine on auto pilot, clueless to what happened.

The tape continues to play—and the head of Video Sam continues to rotate—as the security staff erupts into a fit of laughter. I don't underscore the unfortunate loss of the guest, but it's nonetheless impossible to restrain ourselves.

It could have been any one of us standing there obliviously. It just happened to be Sam's turn, less than a month after retiring as one of New York's Finest.

Opportunities to commit crime usually arise because a guest isn't paying attention at a critical moment. Other times a confident thief randomly chooses a guest, certain that he'll successfully deceive his target. One crook wearing a discarded or stolen doorman's uniform approaches a limo while the real doorkeeper is busy inside. The bogus employee picks up two suitcases, enters the Fifty-First Street entrance and exits through the Madison Avenue courtyard undetected. Another criminal identifies himself as a house officer to a group of women outside the Versailles Ballroom, creating and exploiting a false sense of security by getting close enough to steal a purse from a handbag. Sometimes there's nothing you do to stop such people.

A Hooker Graduates

Out of hundreds of hookers and thieves we encounter over the years, one hustler in particular single-handedly gives us the most trouble. This hooker—I'll call her Belinda—is such a successful thief that she apparently retired from the prostitution trade and instead lived off what she could pilfer. With support from current and former employees of the Palace, she usually slips into the hotel undetected, and more often than not burglarizes rooms without getting caught.

First, a little background information on Belinda for some insight on how an ordinary prostitute can step beyond the limits of "victimless" crime when faced with opportunity and temptation.

She used to operate the same way most other hookers did in this area of Manhattan. Simply put, her customers would *come* and she would *go*.

One reason my predecessors never arrest her for trespassing, or so I'm told, is that half of the security staff accepts sexual favors in return for not busting her. This shady bunch of characters happens to include one guy who later becomes a New York City Police Officer (and is ironically assigned to cover this area of the city) as well as another loser who eventually becomes her lover *and* her partner in crime.

Since she's allowed to roam so freely throughout the hotel, she becomes familiar with the layout of the building—familiar enough to fill its architect with envy. It's unavoidable that such unrestricted access leads her to commit other offenses. This access, combined with her lover's increasing indebtedness to a mob loan-shark who finances his gambling addiction, is the key to their success. It also serves as the main ingredient to their downfall.

The hotel weeds out most of the security personnel who are friendly with Belinda. Others leave of their own accord by time I start working at the hotel. The remaining house officers—the ones who say they don't take favors from Belinda yet remain silent about their coworkers' exploits—swear they want to bust her. However, they try little or nothing to accomplish that goal. I guess it's easier to hear the boss rant and rave about an occasional burglary than it is to remain vigilant nightly and deprive themselves of food and rest.

One night Belinda finds an occupied room with an unlocked door, walks in, and even though the lights are out and the guest is sleeping, manages to find his wallet and jewelry on top of the dresser. It isn't until the next morning that the guest reports the incident, and he reluctantly admits waking up during the burglary.

Unfortunately for all of us, he's too drunk to respond and falls asleep after watching Belinda exit the room. The only reason we know it's her is because of a distinguishing characteristic that a few of her victims, including this one, happen to notice: one of her ankles, which apparently had healed incorrectly after an accident, forces her to walk with a noticeable limp.

We didn't see her coming or going that night, but with such a distinct feature it was safe to assume she's the one.

Until now I never see Belinda in person. It isn't until one of my coworkers points her out to me as she nonchalantly passes by the Fifty-First Street entrance, scoping out the lobby as she does so.

We step outside just to send a message that we're aware of her presence. Surely she won't try to hit the hotel knowing we had spotted her. We return to the lobby.

After walking no more than twenty feet I turn around. There's Belinda, walking in the door almost right behind us, stealthily trying to sneak into the building on the back of our heels. She reverses direction and disappears before we can seize her inside the building. Dragging her back into the hotel is a potential alternative, but we decide to play it safe and wait for another opportunity.

Everyone figures Belinda won't come back for a while. After all, we're so close to nabbing her. She can't be that stupid, or so we thought.

It's business as usual for this slumbering security department. The following morning another guest reports that someone had rifled through his belongings during the night. A notable sum of cash is removed.

As months pass by, the number of burglaries increases. All the guests involved are victimized while sleeping. Apart from that first case which produces a positive ID of Belinda, not one victim detects the crime while in progress. But once or twice a housekeeper or a room service waiter does recall seeing a strange woman limping through the hallway around the estimated time of occurrence.

Belinda continues to elude us, but it's only a matter of time before she screws up. One night I spot her peaking through the Fifty-First Street doors, just like the time she had tried to walk in right behind us. We once again try to track her down, but to no avail.

Perhaps we're better off, because some members of the security team have every intention of giving her a beating. Yes, a trouncing. It isn't right that a couple of grown men are about to take it upon themselves to hit a woman, particularly in the perceived name of justice. But with a lowlife like Belinda causing us so much grief, the situation devolves into an eagerness to punch her in the mouth and drag her back to the hotel against her will.

I'm sure the crew would've simply lied in their incident reports, backing up one another's description of how she went on the attack as they seized her for trespassing. There wasn't much room for fairness or gallantry, some argued.

Fortunately for her (as well as for us, depending on how you look at it) someone is waiting for her in a car down the street from the hotel. She bides enough time for the rage to subside, even if just a little.

By the look on my partner's face I can tell that he recognizes the driver.

"Who the hell was that?" I ask.

"That scumbag!"

"Who? What?"

His jaw hangs open. He turns around and dejectedly walks back toward the hotel, shaking his head in disbelief.

"It was Terry Johnson. He used to be in security. He was one of us."

Now it makes sense how Belinda manages to get into so many occupied rooms. We always find several units with their doors ajar during any nighttime floor patrol. Terry obviously tells her of this frequent oversight by inebriated guests. The odds are in her favor that she can gain access to a room that's occupied by someone who can afford to be there, someone who also can afford to drink themselves to sleep with some of the world's most expensive brandies and cognacs. With targets like these laying around in so vulnerable a position, it's no wonder Belinda keeps coming back for more.

We can't keep her out of the building. Likewise, when she does enter, we're unable to catch her on the way out. Upper management is on the verge of firing the entire security staff because we can't guarantee she won't strike again.

The only thing we can guarantee is that another Palace guest will leave their door open and Belinda is going to find it. But it's this sense of futility that leads to a creative solution, one that finally delivers us to the burglar-whore.

Once again, Belinda wanders the floors of the hotel one night searching for a potential victim, and once again, she finds a door unlocked and a room occupied. With the confidence of a wild animal stalking its prey before the attack, she silently pushes open the door of the darkened room and is about to enter stealthily, undoubtedly expecting to leave with more in her hands than when she arrived. The one variable she doesn't expect, however, is a house officer patiently waiting inside, hoping his assigned room will be her target. Exiting the room before he grabs her, she flees down the hallway.

The other unforeseen development she doesn't anticipate is the fist that seemingly comes out of nowhere, landing on her chin and sending her to the floor. Another officer, I'll call him Benny, responds from the floor above and takes out nearly a year's worth of frustration on this wench. Benny, a wild-eyed ex-Army Ranger known for his explosive temper, continues to smack her around relentlessly in retribution for the embarrassment she had caused our department. His backup arrives and eventually pulls him off her.

Belinda finally is arrested and charged with attempted burglary, criminal trespass and assault, the assault being for her unprovoked attack of Benny when he apprehended her, according to the incident report, that is.

Her partner, Terry, is never apprehended, and even if he was, he would never have been convicted of anything, since Belinda did all the dirty-work. Believe it or not, the last thing I heard about Terry is that he was doing security at some unsuspecting crap-hole of a hotel downtown. If his boss only knew.

I Do Nothing Wrong

A maid, or should I say *room attendant*, as the political-correctness police regularly remind us, retrieves a service cart from housekeeping headquarters in the basement. Slow-rolling wheels squeak in unison every few seconds, as if resisting her efforts to force the cart into the elevator. The housekeeper is a middle-aged South American woman with several years on the job, proud of her union status. Like many of her associate organized laborers, she's militant in manner, wears her perceived job-security like a medal.

She scans the list of assignments on her clipboard, looking up occasionally to respond to a chorus of *holas* from passers by. The pungent yet sanitized odor of industrial-grade cleaning fluids and powders emanates from her cart.

On reaching the twenty-third floor she learns the room at the top of her list is littered with piles of Saks and Bloomingdale's shopping bags and accompanying paper cloth inserts. A half-eaten cheeseburger from room service decays on a tray, competing with the nose-tingling scent of an untouched, ripe onion slice. Three days worth of Wall Street Journals are strewn across either side of the bed, as if separated by a gust of wind that snuck into the chamber from Madison Ave.

There's work to be done, to be sure. But rather than reaching for the tools of the room-attendant trade—a mop, vacuum cleaner, air deodorizer—she descends on a black leather purse on the night table. Like a hawk floating over an open field, a vulnerable rodent in plain view, she snatches a twenty-dollar bill from the purse and shoves it into her cleavage.

Now I'm ready to clean the place, she must be thinking.

She takes her time, whispers thanks to the faceless occupant for leaving a gift. Intermittent smiles and frowns alternately appear on her face. She catches herself bouncing contradictory expressions of anger and gratitude off the bedroom mirror; angry with the unseen individual who dared to leave such a mess for her, yet thankful it provides her with steady work.

The slob she's cursing under her breath isn't some gringo fat-cat millionaire visiting New York on business, however. She soon finds that it isn't even a Palace guest who left behind such filth on the floor, like government officials from Zimbabwe once did for her.

On completion of her chores, she enters the hallway, immediately greeted by a pair of house officers. As far as she's concerned, it's coincidental that security is present.

They tell her, "You're busted," but she's nonetheless unable to grasp how they could know of her thievery. Raising her tone several octaves, she blankets the officers with a barrage of denials, momentarily crippling their ability to respond.

I do nothing wrong. I do nothing wrong, she repeats over and over.

After hearing them describe every move she made over the past hour—the unhesitating penetration of the gaping purse, concealment of the stolen bill, even the little dance she conducted, vacuum in tow—she finally relents. Takes the sweaty twenty out of her bosom. Tears run down her cheek.

Wanting to capitalize on this successful sting, the security chief calls the cops, making sure they escort the maid through the lobby in handcuffs under the watchful eyes of dozens of employees. He achieves the intended effect of spreading word to the hundreds of workers throughout the hotel. But except for key insiders, questions remain. How did security catch her? Wasn't she in a room? How did you guys know what she was doing?

Despite allowing this cloud of secrecy to float among the Palace employees, wafting above their heads like a storm cloud threatening to burst, the deterrent effect of this parade of shame is slight. The only employees heeding the don't-do-the-crime message are the ones who intend to remain honest all along.

Guests in the coming weeks continue to report the "disappearance" of valuables. Some claims are fraudulent, but not all of them. Somebody is committing these crimes, and all signs point to the employees. Hence, the birth of another sting.

A manager directs a bellhop by telephone to bring a newspaper to a rented room, noting the guest was on her way out, granting permission to have the paper dropped off in her absence. Someone at the front desk issues a key to the bellhop. He's on the way to the room, scratching his bald spot, humming a tune from the early seventies.

While inside, without hesitation, he looks inside a purse on the bed, slides his fingers inside, removes a ten-dollar bill, hides it in his pocket.

Before reaching the elevator he realizes he's busted. A Palace employee for nearly a decade, he finds himself surrounded by security, soon to be unemployed. Such an inconvenience. For ten bucks.

The secret? The rooms where we conduct these investigations aren't actually occupied by hotel guests. We simply arrange them to look as if a couple of anal-expulsive travelers had littered Leona's luxury compartments. We choose two bordering units for each sting, one listed in the computer system as O-D (occupied-dirty), another listed as O-DL (occupied-double locked), the latter earmarked to appear off-limits to maids at the request of the supposed guest. The rooms are found on a floor where, statistically, most of the alleged guest losses occur.

To give the O-D room a lived-in look in advance, the guys on the midnight shift intentionally yank the sheets off the bed, throw shopping bags and wet towels on the floor, wheel in a room service cart with dirty dishes, and, most importantly, equip the cable box on top of the television with a hidden video spy camera. We run a wire from the cable converter to a VCR and monitor conveniently located in the O-DL room next door. The boss assigns a house officer to station the room before a targeted work-shift. If an employee takes the bait—usually one bill out of a roll of marked tens and twenties—the officer tells his backup, who then catches the thief who's exiting the crime scene.

Unfair? The only unfairness is the scaring away of potential repeat-customers because of his or her dishonesty. Entrapment, maybe? Try again. First, entrapment doesn't apply to private individuals or companies. State law makes clear that accusations of entrapment are legitimate only when the accused takes the bait when "induced or encouraged to do so by a public servant."

The thieving employee is unable to cry foul. We're not public servants. The law further states that creating the opportunity to commit the crime doesn't mean entrapment has taken place. Taking property that isn't yours is no excuse—even if someone intentionally places the stuff in your view expecting that you'll take it.

Drawing Roaches

Checking the personal bags of all employees as they exited the building is another one of my duties, a tedious, anxiety producing task that I hate to do. Also, the employees, honest and crooked alike, hated having it done. But it's necessary. Simply put, as degrading as the bag-checks seem, they enable us to confiscate pilfered property. One day, it's silverware or crystal. The next, bars of hotel soap, towels, bathroom scales—low-grade crap that *most* people won't risk their jobs over.

Sometimes we seize the items and give the workers a warning, especially if an inspection uncovers thievery on the level of mini-shampoo bottles or a handful of bite-size chocolates. Such warnings are suitably and regularly handed out. Occasionally some rat tips off the boss when go weeks without checking a single package, and then we have no choice but to pop the unsuspecting employee, whose worst offense is bad timing. Catching any thief, no matter how petty the offense, is fair game at this point, regardless if they're stealing commemorative postcards of Mrs. Helmsley or filling their bags with hotel knickknacks.

Our wavering interest in nabbing employees as they passed the time clock is no secret, bordering on predictable. Less obvious to hotel staff is the double standard that management applies to a suspect's resulting termination and/or conviction.

"Bottles were clanking together in his bag, down in the locker room," an ambitious waiter tells me on the phone, referring to a suspicious room-service bartender who's on his way to punch out for the evening. "He's up to no good, I assure you."

Getting a cup of coffee to start off this particular midnight shift is a high priority for me, but the caller threw a hot tip in my lap. I can't delay an inquiry, no matter how badly I need a caffeine fix.

Poised by the employee entrance, standing off to the side where he couldn't see me, I watch the suspect-bartender emerge from the basement stairway among a group of other workers. Every few seconds he looks down at his bag, which he holds stiff-armed, as if for reassurance that no items are protruding.

I've witnessed hundreds of shoplifters and internal thieves in my security career exit that way. The repetitious downward peek was a classic giveaway.

A look of horror appears on his face as I approach him. He closes his eyes, head tilted momentarily, like a dog ready to bow out of a fight. He knows what's coming, but makes a last-ditch effort to weasel out of it.

"Can I see your bag, please?" I ask.

"There are only dirty clothes in this bag," he responds. "You don't want to touch dirty clothes, do you?" He laughs nervously, steps from side to side.

"You're right. I don't," I say.

A glimmer of hope appears on his face, until I continue, "That's why I want *you* to take them out."

Piece-by-piece, he pulls out the laundry. Underneath are two empty glass carafes and a full bottle of Bacardi. I pull the bottle out, raising it for all the other employees to see, and say, "What have we here?"

We escort him to the security office. Unfortunately for him, the assistant director didn't go home yet. The boss, briefcase in hand and cigar in mouth, says, "Call 9-1-1 and have him locked up. I'm tired of this."

The cops arrive, ask a few questions, and arrest him, deservedly so. They take the disgraced employee out through a side entrance, handcuffed.

A similar situation, but with the opposite result, arises a few days later.

A junior chef tries to walk past me without voluntarily opening his bag.

"Open it up, please," I say.

He has an assortment of pots, pans and cooking utensils. No wonder he's trying to breeze right by me. The line of b.s. he blurts out is even more deceptive.

"I don't like leaving this stuff in my locker," he says. "The smell of food draws roaches."

Mistakenly assuming I'd fall for such a false excuse, he takes the frying pan out of my hand. Then he has the gall to stick it back in his knapsack.

However, the pan is wrapped in plastic. It's brand new.

"Nice try," I tell him.

As in the last case of internal theft, our second-in-command happens to be there, and again, he's not in a good humor. So, I figure that this chef will be cooking his next meal in Manhattan Central Booking.

But the boss makes a phone call, then tells the junior chef, almost apologetically, "We're gonna have to hold on to these items until I speak with Chef LaRon tomorrow."

He then says to me, "Get his name and his employee number and write up a report during the night."

Turning his attention back to the chef, he says, "You can go now, but you're suspended until further notice. Call personnel in the morning."

"What do you mean he can go now? Aren't we gonna lock him up?"

"You just do as you're told."

No debate. He just picks up his briefcase and goes home.

Not only does the employee escape arrest, but they allow the twenty-something, white-male Culinary Institute of America graduate to resign the next day. No true record of his misdeed at all.

Julio, on the other hand, had been jailed, prosecuted, terminated.

Some say it isn't a coincidence the employee who gets locked up is Chicano, yet the worker who skates away is white. I can only comment for sure that one of them has connections and the other doesn't. It means all the difference in the world.

Bedbugs and Sledgehammer-Wielding Thugs

As soon as I arrive for work one night, at a quarter to midnight, the assistant security chief flips out. Red-faced and trembling, he shouts, "What the hell are you guys doing here at night? Do you have your heads up your asses or what?"

I stand silently, clueless why he's screaming at me. Not knowing what to say, I blurt out, "Listen…"

"No, you listen to me!" he interjects. "Did you happen to notice that the jewelry store window has a crack bashed in it? Apparently you didn't, because no one bothered to write an incident report about it last night!"

I recall walking past the jewelry store, found inside the lobby, at the end of the previous midnight shift. Can't say for certain whether that I had taken so much as a glimpse at the window. It isn't false, at least in my mind, to say the last time I checked the window it was all right. Armed with a pregnant half-truth, I then deflect the blame onto the day shift.

"That window was fine when I left at eight o'clock yesterday morning."

"You're lucky that they couldn't penetrate that glass. There's three-quarters of a million dollars worth of jewels in that display case alone." He puts a cigar in his mouth and mumbles, "There are gonna be some big changes around here, that's for sure," and slams the door behind him.

He directs the threat of "big changes" at *me*. This is unfortunate, considering I'm perhaps the first person in years to question—and seek to alter—the well-entrenched routine of the midnight security staff. Little does Leona know that each of her Palace guards gets a minimum of three hours of sleep a night, not including the final day of a person's workweek, when he gets a six- or seven-hour break. Having been promoted to relief security supervisor a month earlier, I decide it's a good idea to cut the breaks down to *only* two hours, a decision that does not increase my popularity.

It's risky to slash the number of hours the midnight crew can sleep, considering the pattern has been in place for years. Nevertheless, I take that chance, and it isn't out of a sense of over-eagerness. Rather it stems from a need to provide a *true* sense of security for the guests instead an illusion of it.

True, I had slept the last two hours the night of the attempted smash-and-grab. I didn't realize, however, that when it was *my* turn to disappear, the rest of the security staff would go back to sleep, for the second time in one night, no less.

I revert to three-hour breaks that same night. It's the only way I can ensure, without standing there baby-sitting, that at least one house officer will remain in the lobby. The standard sleep pattern is too well-entrenched on the midnight tour to take it on alone.

Yeah, there'll big changes all right.

It's a common notion in the hospitality industry that employees are the biggest cause of theft. But few people know that it's equally accurate to assign losses, whether suffered by guests or by the hotel itself, to apathy and indifference, not just traditional means of thievery.

Workers unconcerned with the well-being of the hotel and its occupants are no better than those who pilfer in the traditional sense. While we usually targeted certain departments for investigation, such as housekeeping, no one is beyond reproach, including—or should I say *especially*—house security.

Most on the security team were honest people, as were the majority of other Palace employees. But the security staff, myself included, took advantage of the relative authority we were given. Instead of using the sheer number of house officers and uniformed guards available on each tour, particularly on the graveyard shift, as a preventative tool, we abused it, choosing to sleep and eat much more than patrol and observe.

Charlie's Devils

Even when sleeping on the job is detected, it's treated as a house joke. One night, for example, all the rooms are occupied and I'm denied access to a comfortable bedroom. I'm therefore forced to rest on a couch in a chamber of the hotel's historic Villard House. The Library section of the mansion spooks off most sleep-deprived employees, but I resolve to let nothing interfere with my nap.

It's rumored that this section is haunted by a construction worker who was killed there during its renovation in the 70s, a fanciful myth as far as I'm concerned. The supervisor of the metal polisher contractor-crew, who sees me heading in the room's direction, assures me of a visitation from "Charlie," the resident ghost, if I fail to ignore the supposedly troubled spirit.

"I think the fumes from your brass polish are messing up your brain, Victor," I tell the hulking, less-than-brilliant crew leader. "Will *Casper the Friendly Ghost* pay me a visit, too?"

"I'm warning you, it ain't no joke," he says. Continuing in a sing-song voice, he warns, "Charlie's gonna get you!"

I continue up a set of marble stairs, which happen to be lined with sculptures and *bas reliefs* of zodiac figures and gargoyles. The 19th century decorations notwithstanding, I retreat to a leather couch in The Library and doze off with ease.

A few minutes later, the sound of a loud, creaking door wakes me. Ignoring the distraction, I return to my dream state. Must be one of the night cleaners passing through, I assume. No need to worry.

Soon after, the antique, wooden door creaks again, and a beam of light from a stairway lamp shatters the darkness of my chosen sleeping quarters. The entryway, just a few feet from my couch, continues to open wider, ever-so-slightly, but no one appears. Startled by the absence of human movement, I shake my head from side to side to snap out of my slumber. This time, I maintain a constant watch on it, but I'm still groggy. Just as I start to wonder, *Could it be the you-know what?*, the door violently opens and smashes against the wall without a trace of anyone present. Considering the only other possibility, I gasp as I jump to my feet, slowly moving toward the stairway to investigate.

A string, attached to the door handle, runs through the stairwell landing and into the next room. It leads to Victor and his metal-polishing underlings, still positioned on the floor, who upon seeing my chalk-white expression begin flapping on the carpet and convulsing with laughter.

"I told you Charlie was gonna get you," he says.

I Need a Cop... Call the Firehouse

A thirty-something male in jeans and a tee shirt abruptly comes out of the elevator near Harry's Bar. Not just any elevator, but the one leading to the Helmsley's executive offices. He quickens his pace, despite struggling with bulging, weighed-down shopping bags which he grips in each hand.

Unknown to the suspicious individual, my boss and I stand nearby, yearning for the end of the four-to-twelve shift. The boss wants nothing more than to go home, and I'm looking forward to slipping away to room service for a cup of coffee. But we just knew this guy was up to no good. And it wasn't because he was black, either, as one of my coworkers later claimed. He walks towards the exit. The boss and I look at each other, eyebrows raised. Without saying a word we follow him out the door and across East Fifty-First Street.

There's no probable cause to stop him. But by the way he's acting—the quickened pace as he left the building, the frequent glances at the bags, the jerking movements of his head—we can tell there's something in those bags that's not his.

The suspect doesn't stop until he reaches Lexington Avenue, where he places the bags on the floor and leans against a wall to rest. He flinches as we approach.

Jack asks, "Watcha got in the bag, huh? Anything good for sale?"

"I don't know, um, I don't know what you're talking about," he replies.

"I could use some office equipment. How much are you selling that stuff for?" Jack continues to inquire. Jack has no idea what's in the bags. He simply tries his best to call the suspect's bluff to find out.

Unwilling to take the bait, the stranger picks up the bags and flees. An adding machine falls out after his first few steps. I grab one bag from him and see there are various items with the Helmsley Palace logo on them. I run after him, much to Jack's dismay.

"Peacock! Get back here, now. Screw it. Let him run."

I halt my pursuit. The suspect then heads north on Lexington.

"What did you do that for?" I ask. "I almost had him."

"And for all you know he almost had the opportunity to pull out a gun and blow your freaking head off."

"Well, I'm not giving up that easily," I say as I turn and run to the 17th precinct, half a block away.

I sprint into the police station, gasping for breath. A few heads turn, but I don't alarm anyone.

"I'm from Palace Security," I tell the desk sergeant,. "My boss is in pursuit of a burglar right around the corner."

The sergeant looks at a female administrative assistant sitting at the reception desk in front of me. Neither one says a word.

"Hello! Is anybody home?" I ask, baffled at their lack of response. "Excuse me sergeant, do you have an available unit to help us?"

"No. We don't," he says dryly. He then leans over and whispers to the clerk. She dials a number, then tries handing the phone to me.

"Who's this?" I ask, hesitantly reaching for the receiver.

She says, "9-1-1."

I stand speechless for a moment. They stare back, equally mute. As if trying to snap out of a trance, I close my eyes for a couple of seconds, briefly but violently shake my head hard enough to make my cheeks wobble, and then yell, "9-1-1! 9-1-1! You've got to be kidding me! Is this not a New York City police precinct? What kind of crap is this?"

"I suggest you calm down," the sergeant says. "I told you I didn't have anyone available."

"Yeah, you told me you didn't have anyone available after standing there with your jaw hanging open for five minutes."

As I head out the door, I turn and scream, "I should've went to the damn firehouse for help. You people are useless!"

My reference to the firehouse was intentional. A few weeks before this incident, a group of firefighters stationed next to the precinct apprehended an armed robber who ripped off, of all people, one of Manhattan's assistant district attorneys as he came out of the subway.

The Palace technically is in the territory of the Midtown North Precinct, and not of the 17th. The desk sergeant probably views my entreaty for help as an unwanted intrusion into his sector, despite the crime's nearness to his base of operations. More importantly, the sergeant and his crew are probably too lazy to get involved.

Nevertheless, I eventually begin to see why so many professional security and law enforcement officers are discouraged from trying to effect change. Seeing the same offenders breaking the law repeatedly, while watching prosecutors or judges quash arrests for one reason or another, is enough to dissuade the most ambitious security or police officer from giving a hundred percent as the following cases reveal.

You Must Put Fear In Their Hearts

Every Sunday around 5 a.m. a truck pulls up to the Fifty-First Street entrance and drops about a hundred copies of the New York Times onto the sidewalk. The newsstand in the lobby, which is run by an outside vendor, doesn't open until 7 a.m. The owner is too cheap to tip the bellhops for bringing the papers inside the building. The bell staff at one point understandably halts that chore since no one is compensating them for their efforts. Not a single house officer is about to stand guard over anything that isn't hotel property. So, many of the papers—sometimes all of them—"disappear" before the store even opens.

Although initially unconcerned with the situation, we quickly become tired of seeing the same scavengers walking away with bundles of papers every week. I'm not talking about one or two passers by each snagging a free paper to take home. Usually it's a small group of vagrants worked together. They steal the papers in one shot, then sell them at subway entrances throughout the day. One reason I don't bother with them is because I don't want one of these characters following me into the subway station on my way home, seeking vengeance for interrupting his once-a-week source of income.

Eventually we swallow our pride and begin bringing the bundles inside, but even that doesn't work. The scavengers simply come into the lobby and run out the door with them when we're not looking. Then we start chasing them and they usually run away empty-handed. But they overcome this obstacle by seizing the papers seconds after the delivery driver drops them off and pulls away. Tenacious in their pursuit, they even grab them as we bring the papers in. They're persistent, like rats fighting for a piece of cheese.

One night a thief loads up every available Sunday Times—over 100 of them—into a stolen U.S. Postal Service cart and walks away. We apprehend the suspect after a brief struggle in the middle of Park Avenue, bring him to the security office and call the police.

When the cops arrive we insist they arrest the suspect, because of the previous thefts. The two officers, a pair of burly Irish-American cops, look at the cart-full

119

of papers, then at each other. One scratches his head and says, "Our sergeant will kill us if we arrest this guy."

Not the response we expect.

"Officer, please understand that we've been getting ripped off by this guy and his friends every week for months. We have to draw the line."

"I understand what you're saying, but it's the tail end of a crazy Saturday night. All sorts of shit went down on the West Side tonight. If we have to spend the rest of our shift processing this clown and logging into evidence a hundred damn papers, there's gonna be trouble at the precinct."

If we insist on the arrest they'll have little choice but to carry out our request. Then again, giving an ultimatum to police is an unwise undertaking. Sending a message to a low-level thief isn't worth the trouble if it means pissing off the cops we depend on in case of an emergency. Pushing the issue will only haunt us in the long run.

They fill out an incident report. That way, we dissuade the paper thief from accusing us of false imprisonment. We release him.

Juan, one of the midnight-to-eight bellhops, is angered that this could happen.

"This is bull*sheet*," he exclaims, his accent thickening as he grew madder. "In my neighborhood, we know how to take care of scum like this."

"Don't let it bother you, Juan. No one in security is. Not anymore."

He stares back at me, ignoring what I said.

"We will see."

Juan isn't playing around. I know that what he said about how they take care of scum in his neighborhood isn't an idle threat. He comes from the area of Tremont and University avenues in the Bronx, a section that was so bad as far back as the 1960s that my family fled that area for another part of the borough. Just imagine the war zone it is after an another quarter-century of decay. Juan has nothing to lose, and even less to fear.

The following Sunday toward the end of the graveyard shift, still nearly half-asleep as I stand from the lobby couch, I look toward Fifty-First Street and see Juan confronting two men. I later learn that the pair had tried to walk away with the Times—again.

Juan reaches into his pocket then swings at the men in a side-to-side motion. In his hand is a folding knife that's as long as a plumber's wrench. It comes within inches of the thieves' faces. They backpedal furiously as Juan continues his offensive. He's not just trying to scare these guys; he's intent on permanently scarring them.

"Juan! What the hell are you doing?" I yell.

He stares back at me. No reply. I don't push the issue. One of the vagrants, assuming I'm angry with Juan, tries to get on my good side.

"That man is crazy! You're not gonna let him get away with pulling out that knife on us, are you?"

I ask, "What knife?" I then look at Juan. He smiles.

The two thieves finally leave on their own accord. We don't call the cops, and neither do they. Juan and I together bring the papers into the lobby.

"You've gotta be careful, man," I say. "I'd hate to see them become millionaires because you cut off their noses."

Calmly, he adjusts his glasses and says, "You must put fear into their hearts."

I don't agree with his tactics, yet I wonder if I'm if I'm too judgmental; after all, no one tries to take the Sunday papers again for a long time.

Billionaire's Beer

The sound of breaking glass suddenly travels from the other side of the lobby. Outside Harry's Bar, I discover that an unknown person or persons had torn a wall lamp from its foundation and smashed it on the carpet. An elevator door closes nearby, a good sign the suspects are heading towards floors two through five. The elevator panel shows that they get off at the fifth floor. I call for backup and begin my pursuit.

What a way to start New Year's Eve.

On reaching that floor I find that the still-invisible vandals had torn more lamps from the wall. The chase continues, despite not knowing who I was chasing or what I was about to do when I came across the next person.

"There were about five of them," an elderly housekeeper tells me. "They went that way."

She points towards the fire stairwell. When I get there I detect the faint click of a door closing on a floor below. *Which* floor remains a mystery.

Two other house officers catch up with me. We slowly descend the stairs one level, to the fourth floor, which contains a kitchen and several meeting rooms. All clear. We move on to the third level.

Our visitors had knocked down the steel-wire door leading the beer storage area. Missed them again.

Suddenly we hear over the radio, "They ran out the fire exit on Fiftieth Street with about ten cases of beer!"

After a lengthy chase, we seize two of the suspects and return them to the hotel. We recover all the beer, but many bottles broke when the thieves dropped the cases and fled. The police arrest them and cart them away.

One of the cops who responds happens to be a former Palace house dick. He's flabbergasted that we chased these clowns two blocks to nab them.

"Are you crazy?" he asks. "You'd actually risk your life to recover beer that belongs to Leona Helmsley? Think about it. She's a billionaire. Do you think she cares about a few cases of beer? Or about *you*, for that matter? It just ain't worth it."

He's right. No need to feel offended by his reprimand. We were caught up in an adrenaline-induced crisis and let emotion prevail over common sense. We're not even armed. If those guys had been packing pistols, the cops would have been investigating a homicide or two, not a burglary.

About 7 a.m. I go down to the Criminal Courts building. Since burglary is an indictable offense, I need to provide details of the event so an assistant district attorney can draw up formal complaints.

The A.D.A. sits at her desk, a forced smile on her face. As soon as I walk into her office, she says, "Well, I have some good news and some bad news." I brace myself, knowing that such a ridiculous comment means there's only bad news.

"The good news is that you get to go home soon and enjoy a beautiful New Year's Day. The bad news is, no charges can be filed against these alleged burglars."

The obnoxious smile remains plastered on her face, as if her "good news" could make me feel better about having risked my life and wasted my time.

"What the hell do you mean charges can't be filed?"

"First of all, you didn't actually see them breaking into the beer storage room, and…"

"And nothing! We were practically right behind them! A minute after we found the storage room door torn down they were seen exiting the building through a fire exit adjacent to that storeroom!"

She folds her hands. Stays silent.

"What about trespassing? Surely you can't tell me they won't be charged with trespassing. Or can you?"

"There were no signs on the door that said 'no trespassing,'" she says.

"You have got to be kidding me! What about the cases of beer? The broken door? Fleeing the scene? Don't you see the connection here?"

"A good defense lawyer would say in court that they had the beer when they entered the hotel and the broken door was a coincidence."

She pauses before saying, "I've made my decision already. Mr. Peacock, it's a nice day. Why don't you take advantage of it."

"Take advantage of it? I've been working since eight last night! I should be sleeping right now, not wasting my time with you!"

My eyes feel like they're bulging out my head. The lack of sleep and the stale champagne and reefer buzz that's still in my brain doesn't exactly help my mental state. It's insane for her to drop the charges. I respond accordingly.

As I leave her office, I say, "You just want every case handed to you on a silver platter. It's no wonder there's so much crime in this city."

She begins to say something but I cut her off, saying, "Spare me from your bullshit." I'm so disgusted I don't care if she has me arrested. I have to speak my mind, however fruitless the effort.

Before heading home I wander around lower Manhattan getting stoned. This area of the city is desolate, as nearly all the office and government buildings are closed for the holiday. It seems like I'm the last man on Earth, surrounded by endless skyscrapers. One of the few times of the year in the Nation's busiest city that there's not a soul in sight.

Sitting down on a park bench, I look up at an ornate building facade that features a Greek-style image of a woman holding the scales of Justice.

"Yeah, Liberty and Justice for all," I mutter. I feel like laughing, but can't find the energy. I hop on a subway car filled with the by-products, human and otherwise, of another New York City New Year's. *Take me home, Jeeves*, I say out loud to my imaginary chauffeur. No one notices. No one cares.

PART IV
Hookers

Are You Sure You Don't Want a Date?

I cross the intersection of East Fifty First Street and Madison Avenue, in the shadow of St. Patrick's Cathedral. It's my first night on the job. A leggy, blonde wearing a fur coat walks towards me, making eye contact and seductively smiling. She's got high cheekbones, with eyes set wide apart, a facial structure that guys alternately view either as exotic or bizarre. I opt toward exotic. Blushing, however, I'm oblivious to her purposes.

She steps in my path, brushing against me while grabbing my shoulder to slow my pace. She brings me to a halt in the middle of Madison. Northbound traffic stops one block down, thanks to a well-timed red light. We stand in the crosswalk, but only long enough for her to ask, "Do you need a date tonight?"

"No, not tonight," I respond with a hint of naivete, continuing on my way.

She changes direction and walks alongside me, still smiling. Her perfume is strong, but stimulating. After running her right hand along my left suit-sleeve, from shoulder to the biceps, she drops her fingers to my crotch, grabbing a handful and asking, "Are you sure you don't want a date?"

I later explain to my new coworkers what had happened, expecting them to be as shocked as I was. They look at one another and grin.

One of the guys, a retired cop from the Bronx, asks, "Was it a tall, blonde bimbo wearing a mink?"

"In fact it was," I say. "How the heck did you know?"

"That's Bambi. She's been peddling her rear-end between here and the Waldorf for years. It won't be the last time you see her."

"Don't they ever lock her up?"

"Sometimes. I've had her arrested so many times that I can't be bothered anymore. I just throw her out."

"So what should I do if I see her in the hotel?"

"Bring her in here and have her arrested."

"But I thought you just said it's a waste of time?"

"It is, if you do it repeatedly. But since you're new here and you already know what one of the regulars look like, you might as well take advantage of it. If the security chief sees that you're making apprehensions so soon, he'll stay off your back for a while. He'll give the paperwork to the general manager to show that the boys on the midnight shift aren't sleeping all night. The G.M. stops bothering our boss, and our boss stops bothering us. It's all a game.

"You can't be gung ho about busting hookers," he adds. "It's like shoveling shit against the tide, if you know what I mean."

I soon learn that the prostitution trade is flourishing in New York, despite a rise in sexual anxiety stemming from the AIDS epidemic.

Call Girls and Streetwalkers

From 1987–1992 B.G. (Before Giuliani), you could take a stroll through any of the hotel districts in Manhattan after dark and find hookers readily available. Even if you couldn't find one hustling in the open, all you had to do was turn on channel 35 (then courtesy of Manhattan Cable) and scan through dozens of advertisements for "escort services." The ads stopped short of saying, "Have your credit card ready, make your request and wait for us to deliver a whore to your door. Operators are standing by."

White and Black, Latino and Asian, male and female, straight, gay, transvestite and even transsexual hustlers seemingly are at your disposal in the Big Apple. From the perspective of a midnight house detective, one could see that people from all over the world came to New York with the goal, whether as a primary or secondary consideration, of buying or selling flesh.

Just take your pick and bring them back to the hotel, folks. Or at least try to.

The Palace was a veritable magnet for criminal activity, since most hookers were drawn to its cash-rich customers as a matter of economics. Responding to demand, the girls provided a supply. Similarly, the visibility of this supply sparked a demand from intoxicated, lust-filled guests.

Other girls were less entrepreneurial than they were opportunistic, often robbing their victims after selling—or in *pretense* of offering—sexual satisfaction.

There are only two types of prostitutes: call girls and streetwalkers. The call girls always show up in a cab or a private car chauffeurs them to the hotel. Many are gorgeous. Most, at best, are decent looking or marginally attractive, and work for agencies that send them all over the metropolitan area for a $250 hourly minimum. If the hooker is beautiful or has an outrageous body, she charges $500, $1,000 or even $1,500 an hour.

Call girls rarely, if ever, rip off their customers. No wonder, considering the going rate. Their agency bosses further discourage thievery by the fact that such organizations are notoriously mob connected. Do you think it's a coincidence the police occasionally identify dismembered bodies found stuffed in suitcases and left in bus terminal rental lockers, and bloated corpses found floating in the East River as known prostitutes? This isn't to say that these women don't suffer at the hands of murderous sadists, who no doubt take advantage of the vulnerability of the girls' positions, job-wise and horizontal-wise. Skimming profits and scaring away repeat customers often leads to career-ending brutality.

The typical routine for hookers of the street-level variety is to venture by foot from Lexington Avenue, the heart of the East Side hotel district. Others arrive in their personal cars which, for some reason or another, almost always have New Jersey license plates.

Some might fit into the attractive category. Most are skeletal hounds in need of a blood transfusion and a few hearty meals. Others are candidates for liposuction or some other drastic measure.

Regardless of how they get to the Palace, they either circle the hotel like vultures in flight or go straight to Harry's Bar in the hotel lobby, waiting to get picked up by a drunk who doesn't mind crawling between the legs of a cross-eyed and toothless streetwalker.

The Farmer's Daughter

To limit hooker access to the hotel, especially during the first few hours of the midnight shift when guests were more intoxicated and vulnerable, we set up a sign by the elevator that reads, "Please Show Your Key Before Entering Elevator." The keys, which are thin pieces of paper and foil, three inches wide and five inches long, help us to distinguish who is a registered guest from those who are not. The visibility of the sign also covers our ass just in case a legitimate guest gets insulted or feels discriminated against if we stop him or her

This system of checking keys was not without its faults, however.

One particular woman walks toward the elevators, and although she has a key in her hand, she seems a bit uncomfortable. On questioning her it's revealed the guest she wants to visit gave her a duplicate key outside the hotel, where he told her to meet him on the twenty-ninth floor, down the hallway from his room. Unfortunately for her, she doesn't know his name or his room number. Therefore, we can't corroborate her claim that a guest is expecting her.

They then have the cops arrest her for trespassing. And because she can't prove why she has a hotel key, they also charge her with possession of a burglar's tool.

Since we don't check the keys of every person that walks past us, at first I'm confused about whom I should stop and question. I ask one of the more experienced house officers how to use my discretion in weeding out prostitutes. He says: "Most normal women come into the hotel at this time of the night with a male acquaintance or a group of family members. Only a sicko or a no-good whore roams the city by herself at this hour. When you see a woman heading towards the elevator alone, carrying a shoulder bag the size of a small fish-tank, ask yourself the question, 'Would my mother or my sister be doing this?'"

I eventually develop a sixth sense in discovering whether to approach somebody. Sometimes it takes no more than a glance to decide which woman (and even which men) are hustlers. Some try much too hard to fit in, to the point of sending out vibes that ring of discomfort, silently screaming out that they're not as at ease as they wish.

Most of the hookers at the Palace aren't the stereotypical dirtbags you see in the movies. It's rare that a tall-haired, gum-chewing hoe in a ultra-mini skirt

131

walks through the door. On the contrary, many of them come to the hotel look-ing like "The Farmer's Daughter," as I call it, wearing full-length, conservative dresses and shirts buttoned up to the neck. They remind me of the limited edi-tion collectible dolls you see advertised in the magazine section of any Sunday paper.

The way they dress throws me off at first, but by the expressions on their faces as well as the giant shoulder bags that they carried, I always pick them out.

If someone tries to get on the elevator without showing a key, I politely ask him or her to produce one. If they don't have a key, yet know the room number and the last name of the person they want to see, I call the guest and ask if they're expecting a visitor. Unfortunately, most guests respond in the affirmative, know-ing there's not much I can do if they indeed say *yes*.

When a *visitor* doesn't know the last name of the guest, however, I'm able to apprehend her. But I usually opt to let her call their agency and find out the full name of the customer. If they cop an attitude with me, I make them use the pay phone at the corner of Fiftieth and Madison, just to make their job a little more difficult.

Walking to the corner, especially after midnight in the middle of winter, is an annoyance, and not just because the wind is whipping up their skirts and freezing their private parts. More importantly, it makes them a few minutes late for the rest of their appointments that evening. Time is money, even more so in the sex industry than other employment sectors.

Suggesting suspicion during my phone inquiry is particularly effective when the john isn't from the U.S. Unaware that hotel security doesn't have the same power as the Internal Security Directorate of their oppressive home countries, they panic and deny that they're expecting anyone.

"Hello, Mr. Abdul? This is house security. There's a woman here in the lobby that says her name is Mary and that you're expecting her." I pause before asking, "Is that true?"

Usually there's silence for a moment, or a lengthy and uncertain, "ahhhh, ummmm," followed by outright denial.

"I do not know what you are talking about. I do not know a woman named Mary. Do not let her in."

"Thank you Mr. Abdul."

At this point I have every right to detain the hooker, even if only to give her a formal warning for trespassing. I call the cops only if our records show we flagged her previously.

According to the Criminal Code of the State of New York, an individual is trespassing when they "enter premises with no lawful right to do so." When "Mr. Abdul" denies that he knows the woman, it gives me probable cause to catch her. She had no recourse since, technically, she illegally entered the place.

What could she do, go to court with an invoice showing that Mr. Abdul called *1-800-BlowJob* that night? Maybe in Vegas, but not in the Big Apple.

Encouraging hookers to find out the name of their customers backfires on us once, however.

My Wife? My Wife Is In Tokyo!

Hours after a whore services a guest, she goes to Le Trianon, the hotel's main restaurant, and identifies herself as the man's wife, Mrs. Noguchi. Despite being Caucasian, the manager has no reason to doubt her claimed identity. The name she gives matches the room number on the computer printout.

She devours an entree. Then an appetizer and a dish of caviar. She washes it all down with two consecutive bottles of wine. An escape is potentially easy, since the restaurant automatically charges the five-hundred dollar tab to her so-called husband's room.

However, she falls asleep at the table.

The waiter is unable to wake her. The manager calls Mr. Noguchi in his room and asks him to retrieve his wife from the restaurant.

"My wife?" he responds, "My wife is in Tokyo! What are you talking about?"

He rushes downstairs to see what's going on. Sprawled out among the dirty dishes is the hooker he banged not an hour before. N.Y.P.D. arrests her for theft of services, among other charges. Mr. Noguchi is "forgiven" for the bill. The hotel eats the loss.

The easiest way for a hooker to circumvent the key check system is to walk in with the guest that's patronizing her (or him, or *it*). If the suspected prostitute hadn't been warned previously to stay out, and she's currently accompanied by a registered guest, I usually let them pass without saying a word.

That doesn't leave me without an alternative, however.

I nonchalantly get on the elevator with them, waiting until they press the button for the floor they're going to. At that point, I press the button of a higher floor so they don't think I'm following them. When we arrive at their destination, I stay in the compartment for a moment. I wait until they walk away from the elevator bank, then tiptoe across the floor, waiting and listening for them to open the room door. Since the elevators aren't visible from most rooms, they can't see me sneaking around. As soon as I hear the click of the door, I peek my head around the corner and note which room they enter.

This effort enables me to keep track of people each hooker visits over time. I make an entry in the security log book, something to the effect of, "12:30 a.m.;

escorted guest and visitor to room #1426." The hooker usually leaves exactly one hour later; then a second log entry is made: "1:30 a.m.; visitor to room #1426 exited hotel." Since I may not know the hooker's name yet, I make a mental note of who she is and what she looks like.

Over weeks or months a hooker repeatedly returns with an assortment of men. I then check the log and verify that the prostitute, say her name is Charlotte, had visited Mr. Smith for an hour on April 12th, Mr. Johnson for an hour on May 29th and Mr. Salaam for an hour on June 1st.

However, when Charlotte comes back a third or fourth time—when it's beyond a reasonable doubt that she's hustling—I don't document her arrival. Instead, I let her go upstairs and wait until she comes back down. Only then do I ask if she's a guest. After she replies 'no' I ask about who she's visiting.

Chances are, Charlotte can't recall the room number, the guest's name, or either. Without resistance from the woman, who by now realizes she's boxed in, I apprehend her for trespassing.

Another hypothetical scenario entails Charlotte remembering the guest's name and his room number. She gets belligerent, thinking she's getting over. I recite the list of who she's been visiting, including the date and time. I bring her to the security office, take her picture and warn her not to return. If she comes back after that, I detain her once again, call the police, and she ends up in central booking until she's arraigned by a judge the following morning.

It isn't just the hookers giving us difficulty. Sometimes it's the guests themselves making the biggest commotion in response to our efforts.

Once, Twice, Three or Four Times (With) a Lady

A woman that's table-hopping in Harry's Bar is under surveillance. It doesn't take long before she catches the attention of some guy and eventually goes up to a room with him. Since I'm not yet one-hundred percent sure she's a hooker, I don't bother following them. There's the possibility that she's just a horny guest looking to get laid rather than *hired*.

She comes back to the bar a little while later, repeats the routine. After fishing around from table to table, all which are attended by lone men, one bites. She travels upstairs with him. She returns to the Harry's one more time, finds a third prospect.

This time, however, I intervene, stopping them before getting on the elevator.

"I'm sorry, sir. This woman isn't allowed in the hotel," I say.

His response? Drunken fury.

"I'll bring whoever I damn well please to my room!" he hollers, approaching as if about to hit me. His lungs dump oxidized alcohol into the air. His breath is like wet-dog odor. "I'm paying three-hundred and fifty dollars a night for this room and I'll be damned if I listen to you!"

"Sir, she's not going upstairs," I say, taking a step back to avoid the stale whiskey fumes. Keeping my distance seems like a good idea also because although an older man, he's about six inches taller with shoulders as wide as a kitchen table. He's drunk, towering over me, and I'm the only thing preventing him from busting a nut with a young whore.

"Get me someone who knows what the hell they're talking about," he demands. "I want your supervisor."

The boss, who was with me earlier when we first starting watching the hooker, arrives soon after. I try to explain what's going on. The guest tries shouting over our conversation.

"What kind of bull…!"

My boss turns and replies, "Okay, sir, you can take her upstairs now if you want."

The guest sneers, a wry smile appearing in a silent display of victory. He's about to take the hooker by the hand and head toward the elevator. Until, however the boss continues, "You can take her upstairs, yeah, no problem. Apparently you don't mind that you're the fourth guy that she's gone up with this evening, and I don't mind that either. But when she puts a couple of knockout drops in your drink, and you wake up two days later and see that all your belongings have been stolen, you'll realize why this man was trying to stop you."

The guest pauses to think.

"Get rid of her," he mumbles before stumbling to the elevator.

We let the woman go with a verbal warning. No need to push the issue. Just go.

Such incidents are so frequent that I develop a standard speech for dealing with the uncooperative, whether guest or prostitute.

For instance, say a hooker tries to walk by me to get on the elevator. First, I ask to see her room key, which I know she doesn't have.

The resistance builds as follows:

"I don't have a key. I'm just visiting a friend."

"Well, what's your friend's name?"

"Tom."

"Tom what?"

"I don't know."

"Waddaya mean *I don't know*?"

"I don't know."

"What room is he staying in?"

Fifteen twenty-three."

"But you don't know Tom's last name?"

"I told you, no."

She gets a bit flustered, just where I want her. She's cornered, but I provide a way out.

"Let me tell you something. You just tried to get on the elevator and you can't even tell me who you're supposedly visiting. Technically, you're trespassing Now, keep in my mind that I can have you arrested if I choose to do so, but I'm in a good mood tonight and I'm gonna give you a choice."

I stare at her and nod, to see if we're on the same wavelength. She nods in response. The old salesman trick works. Say 'yes' or nod enough times and your target likely will do the same.

"Now we can do this easy way or the hard way, the easy way being my way, which is you come to the security office, I take a mug shot, you give me your name and address and then you go your merry way, no police involved."

I switch gears. Pull my own, *good cop-bad cop* routine.

"Now if you don't want to cooperate," I continue, "I'll drag your stupid ass to the office anyway and then you'll go to jail."

I stand silently, looking her straight in the eye without blinking, like a broker handing a pen to a prospective client. Close the deal, sign-the-dotted-line silence. She nearly relents, so I break away from the sales approach. "So, what's it gonna be, the hard way or the easy way?"

"All right, all right," she say. "I'll cooperate. Just hurry up. I've got other appointments to keep."

They never resist after hearing this barrage of subtle threats. Never once in five years do I have to get physical with any of them. No doubt I give the impression I might wrestle them into the office if they don't voluntarily start walking. Little do they know I have no intent of putting a hand on them. It just isn't worth the aggravation.

The Tide Returns

Hookers and johns become wise to our key-check system, which do doubt interrupts, but hardly halts, their activities. Some take great pains to avoid the process.

A woman comes through the Fifty-First Street entrance and heads into Harry's Bar. She reminds me of a hooker I once busted, but I can't say for sure. She's with five drunken men who appear to be in their twenties. Rather than stopping in for cocktails, they traverse the lounge and come out the other side. They enter an elevator adjacent to the bar.

A couple of the guys alternately look over their shoulders, as if concerned somebody might be tailing them. Plus, the compartment they get is designated to service the banquet halls and corporate offices. This combination of suspicious body language and out-of-character routing silently communicates the group's true designs to me. The second-floor bathroom might be their destination, but I have a feeling that they have something else in mind; namely, to sneak into the other set of elevators. Accessible from the mezzanine, this route circumvents the lobby security checkpoint and creates an alternate means of access to guest floors eight through thirty-nine.

As I expected, they choose the alternate route. I run up the grand staircase, catching up with them after they've already gotten into elevator number two. The men are surrounding the suspected hooker in a semi-circle, some ogling, some grinding.

Unexpectedly to them, I wave my hand between the closing doors, triggering the reopening sensor. As the bronze panels slide back in the wall, their toothy, contorted grins turn tight-lipped and horizontal, like a sudden flat-line on a hospital cardiac monitor. Not until I identify myself do they realize I'm not a robber, call girl agency enforcer or jealous husband.

They return to relax mode. One of the males produces his key, then quickly slips it into his inside jacket pocket. With the overconfident tone typical of a seasoned trial attorney, he bids me good night, as if saying, "Go away, little boy. Play somewhere else." Undeterred, I continue my inquiry, asking, "What about you, miss. Are you registered here?"

"She' a friend of ours," someone from the rear of the compartment answers, "and she's coming upstairs."

I know that this woman is a hooker, but I can't place where I had seen her before. By time I decide to take action, the doors begin to close. I don't feel like forcing them open. Besides, these guys are intent on pulling a train on this young blonde hottie, and I lack the energy to dissuade them.

It later hits me that the blonde is Bambi, the hooker that grabbed my crotch my first night. Months had passed. I didn't recognize her.

I'm furious with myself for letting an easy apprehension fall through. I'll wait for her to come down .Have this sneaky hooker arrested.

Later in the evening, while patrolling the Fiftieth Street side of the lobby, I watch Bambi stroll out the entrance—at the opposite end of the corridor. I can't get mad. Instead, I blurt out a loud chortle, laughing at how I got so worked up in the first place. The advice of one of the old-timers in my department on not being gung ho in busting hookers echoes through my head: *It's like shoveling crap against the tide*, he always says. *It just keeps on coming back at you.*

Despite an increasing number of guests getting ripped off during prostitution-related encounters, most of the hookers seem interested only in selling their wares and leaving quietly. All the while, most try their best not to heap more conflict on top of their risky duties. Some know a guest has to give clearance by telephone before going to a room unescorted. Rather than trying to slip by undetected, they immediately provide the name of the guest and wait patiently to have their information verified.

A few thank me for not giving them a hard time, some of whom I eventually see so often that I decline to ask where they're going. They perform their duties without causing me any grief. In return, I make believe I don't see them.

This unwritten policy continues until one hooker compromises my trust, putting knockout drops in a guest's drink and nearly killing him.

Drop-Dead Knockouts

Suzy, standing in at 5'11 and weighing more than 250 pounds, seems like the typical happy hooker. All the workers in Harry's Bar know her. More importantly, they like her. Manny the bartender says she's polite and tips well. She never resorts to table-hopping in search of business, according to Sophie the waitress. And there's never an inkling of suspicion that Suzy rips off guests or wanders the hotel beyond where she picks up and services her clients.

I usually try to dissuade prostitutes from entering the hotel, especially if they spend a lot time in Harry's or the Hunt Bar. But when it comes to Suzy, with her round face and childlike smile, I'm never compelled to bother her. Sure, I let my guard down with her, but never feel uncomfortable doing so.

Suzy, despite her obesity, has a cute face and enormous breasts—her most effective marketing tools. Hotel guests that spend time in Harry's, whether for post-business unwinding or specifically searching for sex, usually want no part of her. But she has tenacity. More than a few guests take her for a whirl, likely because of the hugeness of her chest. It may be the only thing that keeps her in business. In a way, she's a freak of nature. Some guys like that in a woman.

I see Suzy go up to a room one Saturday night with a tiny, foreign-looking man. Walking alongside her, he's easily half her size. He's nearly drooling on his $2,000 Italian suit, looking eager to have a pair of droopy double-E cups wrapped around his head.

She leaves the hotel less than an hour later, quietly. As usual, she's smiling.

I don't know it at first, but she has a reason to smile. Two days later, on Monday, the patron in question wakes up from a drug-induced near-coma, minus a $25,000 Rolex watch.

Suzy recognized an opportunity and seized on it. Luckily, I didn't document that I saw her go upstairs with the victim.

Suzy's lapse into thievery made everyone's life difficult. Not just for the guy that lost his diamond and ruby-studded Rolex, but more so for the midnight security staff and the "legit" whores who didn't bother anyone. Every manager from the top on down despised us for "allowing" this to happen, even though the incident never made it to the media. If the theft had made it to print, we would've found ourselves on the unemployment line.

The result is that all the girls wind up paying for Suzy's crimes. As the saying goes, *shit rolls downhill.* The executive manager threatens the security chief, who then takes it out on the midnight crew. As a result, we take it out on every whore that comes into the hotel. We have to send a message to Whoredom that it is isn't business as usual at the Palace.

The drug scopolamine (pronounced Sco-PAH-LUH-meen) is an animal tranquilizer that prostitutes occasionally use to incapacitate their customers before robbing them. According to an N.Y.P.D. Hotel Crimes Squad bulletin, one or two drops of this drug in your drink are enough to knock out an average-sized man. Two or three drops put some people in a coma-like state for more than a 24-hour period. A few more than that kills you.

Guys that get ripped off always, and I mean *always*, have drinks with the hooker. This baffles me. Spending hundreds of dollars to have sex with a barely attractive hooker is bad enough. But to bring one to a classy hotel and buy her drinks? It's dangerous to allow a total stranger to enter your room, but then to leave your drink unattended with that person? Even more bizarre is their choice of drinks. Not only are some johns seeking a sexual outlet, but they also display a need to impress prostitutes with their knowledge of, or just their ability to buy, expensive wine or champagne. Some have a lot of cash to spare or have impressive corporate titles, but otherwise they're social cripples.

One buffoon of a guest actually buys a $1,500 bottle of French wine to drink with a woman who he paid $250 to give him a blow job! Then she robs him, giving him too much scopolamine and nearly committing homicide in the process.

I've been unable to figure out what these johns are thinking when they provide such opportunities to prostitutes. But I've pieced together, step by step, a sequence of events that usually leads to getting slipped a mickey.

Picture this: A man flies to New York on a business trip. He goes straight to the bar upon his arrival at the hotel. He can either be single or married, and he's hundreds, if not thousands of miles from home. While sitting at the bar he polishes off a few drinks and is feeling lonely. The more he drinks the less inhibited he becomes. A sly whore who's been scanning the bar sees the man and sits on the stool next to him. She strikes up a conversation. If she's really slick, she waits for him to speak first.

The next step involves one of two possible scenarios, one being more devious than the other. The first option is for her to drop a hand into his lap, making no bones about the fact she's a hooker, advising him she'll perform oral sex for a certain sum. The other possibility is for the woman is to approach the lonely drunk, act cute and sexy and arouse the guest without laying a hand on him. Her sweet comments, mixed with seemingly sincere passiveness, are flattering, not intimidating.

The man is middle-aged, possibly elderly, and is insecure about his appearance. Nevertheless, the woman tells him how sweet he is, how good-looking he may be (whether true or not) and he absorbs her flattery more quickly than a pimply teen.

A couple of compliments and cognacs later and then she whispers in his ear: I want you.

On the way to his suite he decides between a blow-job or a lay. His defenses are down and his pecker is up, depending on the extent of his drunkenness. He orders a couple of drinks from room service and the whore waits for the chance to pull out her bottle of scopolamine. Maybe she puts a few drops in his drink while he relieves himself in the bathroom. Perhaps she puts it in as he wobbles around the room incoherently.

Regardless, he eventually sips on a drink containing a substance normally used only to subdue large animals. She may take his Rolex and nothing else. Or, as I had seen on one occasion, she might take as much as she can possibly hold, including his luggage, the towels and all the toilet paper.

I imagine that some of these women have the mentality that enables them, quite consciously, to squirt in a large enough dosage to bring their victims to the brink of death. By doing so, it gives them more time to flee the scene and hide or sell the stolen property, long before someone reports the crime, if it's ever reported at all.

Most of the victimized guests are understandably embarrassed, particularly if they're corporate executives or hold a high-profile position somewhere, and are unwilling to testify in court.

Surprisingly, the crime that their assailant is usually charged with isn't as serious as one might expect. And technically, the thief isn't using physical force before taking possession of the guest's valuables. Instead of charging her with robbery, the district attorney's office slaps the perpetrator with theft and assault charges.

The way the law is worded at the time, officials can accuse a suspect of robbery or attempted murder only if the victim ingests enough scopolamine that he nearly dies. In the end, the DA always offers a plea bargain for a less serious crime, and the thieving whore does little, if any, time behind bars.

This is exactly what happens to the only hooker we catch for such an act during my five years at the Palace.

The victim is typical of the assumed profile I described earlier. He's a businessman, I believe from Denmark or Sweden, middle-aged, married, doing business thousands of miles away from home.

Much more business than his wife or employer were aware of, certainly.

When he wakes from his deep sleep he discovers most of his belongings are missing, including, not surprisingly, a Rolex watch. He then calls security. The responding house officer jots down a description of the perp and an approximate time of occurrence. Although the victim remembers what the suspect looks like, he's off the mark when it comes to the time and date.

He says he met the woman yesterday, meaning Monday, but has no idea that it's now Wednesday. He goes to the hospital and is treated and released.

When he comes back to the to the hotel, the cops ask if he'll recognize his assailant if he sees her. Since he had picked her up on Fiftieth Street near the Waldorf, an area once notorious for its concentration of prostitutes, he agrees to take a ride. Perhaps she's stupid enough to return to that spot, the detective hopes.

Sure enough, she's on the corner where the victim originally picked her up.

Although they arrest her and charge her with robbery and attempted murder, the Manhattan D.A.'s Office later offers her a plea bargain. She pleads guilty to lesser charges and avoids a trial that potentially could, but unlikely will, send her to prison for years. It *seems* that justice isn't being served, but after all, the Nordic John won't return to New York months later to testify and ultimately reveal to the world that he patronizes hookers. The hustler in question therefore gets a slap on the wrist. It's better than nothing, but she's probably still hustling. Still robbing, too.

Alcoholism, or at least drunkenness and drug-use, are major contributors to the existence of prostitution and the crimes of opportunity committed in conjunction. It's a rare instance to see a sober man going to his room with a hooker. More often than not, johns don't have the faculties one might otherwise have when faced with such a decision—a decision whose outcome, at the least, is penetrating an orifice of some freak they've never seen before.

This doesn't mean that sober men never patronize hookers. It's just that, based on my observations, most street-level whores are repulsive. Without the lack of restraint that comes with intoxication, such unattractive women couldn't possibly make a living in that line of work. The following is a prime example of how only an inebriated person gets intimate with a prostitute of the lowest variety.

Johnny Scissorhands

A guest from the hotel wanders around midtown one evening searching for a hooker. He picks one out and tries to bring the individual back to his room. When they get to his floor, the hooker puts a pair of scissors to his jugular vein, demanding his wallet and jewelry.

"Give your money, or I'll kill you. I'll stab you right in the neck if you yell."

The guest resists, somehow escapes injury. The hooker panics and runs down the fire stairwell with the guest in pursuit.

By opening the ground level emergency exit door the hooker trips an ear-piercing alarm. Two house officers, stationed nearby, give chase and seize the suspect almost a block away on the steps of St. Patrick's Cathedral. The hooker first puts up a fierce struggle, wildly swinging the scissors and nearly catching one of my coworkers in the throat. The resulting scuffle results in a severe beating of the hooker, whose clothing they unintentionally tear as they battle to put on the handcuffs.

One thing becomes obvious at this point: the hooker isn't a woman. Unknown to the guest, it's a man, a transvestite.

I later recognize who, or should I say *what*, it was. This transvestite, whom I had seen venturing around the hotel in the past, obviously is diseased, both physically and mentally. The sores on his face, hands and legs suggest he's either suffering from AIDS, shooting dope, or both. One might think that such ghastly physical features, besides the haunting, faraway look in his eyes, are enough to scare away the average person looking for contact comfort. This clearly isn't enough to scare away the drunken fool who ended up with a pair of scissors at his throat.

Go Ahead. Take Her Upstairs

A middle-aged but well-endowed blonde wearing a red, cleavage-revealing dress walks into Harry's Bar from the Fifty-First Street side of the lobby. She zigzags her way through an arrangement of small tables, obviously eyeing potential clients. Takes just a few seconds for me to figure out she's a hooker, though I doubt many other people even notice her, except the bartenders. They're just as adept as house security in knowing who doesn't belong. Con-artists, druggies, prostitutes, you name it, with just a glance, maybe a minute of observation at the most, we can spot such hustlers. It's almost as if they're trying just a little too hard to fit in. It's behavior, not dress, that gives them away. After a while one gets a sense that some people are up to no good.

Like most hookers that come into the Palace, this particular woman doesn't dress like a sleazeball, despite what Hollywood would have you think otherwise. Except for a lack of concern that her bra is peaking out of her blouse, she's nearly a carbon copy of seven other Manhattan businesswoman in Harry's.

However, several indicators are amiss. None mean anything on their own, but collectively provide a textbook description of a prostitute working a joint. First, she's sitting at the far end of the bar, a spot that every hooker picks when they can. That way she's visible to a greater number of onlookers, and can view the place in its entirety. This increases the odds of contacting a john. Second, she orders a soda—the cheapest available item—and lets it sit there for a long time; the purchase removes any immediate justification to send her packing. Plus, she makes regular eye contact with all the men. One might argue that she's looking for a one-night stand, but I know that's not the case. Although I'm sure a few hookers slip by me throughout five years of trying to identify them, every one that I judge to be a prostitute—without fail—turns out to be a prostitute.

The opposite end of the bar serves me well in carrying out surveillance. I sit there sipping a soda, yapping with the bartenders. Talking and watching. It doesn't take long before a tall, good-looking, well-dressed forty-something guy looks from left to right before handing her cash. During the transaction we make eye contact. Worse, I swing my head away, solidifying any suspicion he may have that he's being watched. He whispers in her ear, and they exit the hotel. They walk about half a block, to the corner of Fifty-First and Park Avenue, where they hail a cab.

Out of curiosity I return to Harry's to check the man's bar tab. His name, and more importantly, his room number, are on the receipt. He *is* a guest, after all. Why in the world does he get in a cab with the hooker?

I have a hunch to go to the other side of the lobby. I stare out the door, patiently waiting for their arrival. A few minutes later, their cab pulls up to the curb. I smile.

They reenter the lobby and try to get on the elevator.

"Nice try," I say. "Why don't you step off to the side and get a refund from your, um, 'friend.'"

Knowing he's busted, yet given an opportunity to back out of an otherwise embarrassing situation, I'm sure he'll panic, maybe even walk away and abandon his deposit. Not a chance.

"Are you implying that something funny is going on around here?" he asks confidently.

Unwavering, I say, "I think the word 'pathetic' would apply."

Wide-eyed and without hesitation he marches to the front desk and demands to see "someone in charge." The night lobby-manager, Hector, briefly listens to the man's belligerent rant. I stand nearby, ready to explain the situation. Within seconds, after simply hearing that I refused entry to the guest's "friend," Hector says to him, "Go ahead. Take her upstairs."

"What the hell do you mean he can take her upstairs?" I ask.

The guest smirks, turns on his heel and heads toward the elevator, hooker in tow.

"I'll be waiting for you when you come down," I tell the woman. Surely she won't remember the guest's name, or even what room she visited. I'll then bust her for trespassing, since she won't be able to contact anyone to vouch for her.

Turning my attention back to the manager that overrode my decision I demand an explanation.

"Did it occur to you that maybe I had a reason for stopping her?" I ask.

His response?: "If you want to play superhero, that's your problem. I can't be bothered."

An hour later the guest returns to the lobby with the hooker, holding hands, no less. He escorts her to a cab outside, like a couple of kids on a date. The taxi pulls away and the arrogant john walks back to the elevator. He glances at me with a snide look. He wins. We both know it.

Harry's closes, the lobby is suddenly vacant, and I stand there, with way too much time to think. I pace the lobby, wondering whether I'm wasting my time trying to keep hookers out of the hotel.

I must have busted more than a hundred hookers for trespassing. Never did I think for a second that I'd stem the flow, but I wasn't going to make it easy for them.

"If these guests are so intent on screwing around with hookers, shouldn't I just look the other way when they come in?" I ask myself. "What's the point? If they want to risk getting robbed by some opportunistic streetwalker, why bother trying to deter them?'

I'm beaten down emotionally. The game of Catch-the Hooker just isn't the same after this, and this feeling of defeat becomes progressively worse.

Look At It This Way...

Most of my coworkers ignore the flow of prostitutes long before I start to get discouraged. One of the other house officers, Tim, asks why I was so intent on keeping track of the parade of hookers in and out of the hotel.

"Because they keep ripping off the guests," I say. "If we're lax, it'll only get worse."

"I just don't give a damn," Tim says. "If they get ripped off, well, they get ripped off. That's just the chance they take. The dummies ask for it, leaving themselves wide open. Besides, the supply simply meets the demand. Oldest profession in the book, all that."

Instead of snoozing for a few hours, we decide to take our *lunch break* outside the hotel. It's okay to leave the building to get a few beers. After all, there are two other people from security that are keeping an eye on things while we were gone. What's the difference? We would've been sleeping anyway, we reason.

About 1 a.m. we walk to the nearest deli, two blocks away on Lexington Avenue, and pick up a couple of quarts of beer. While wandering the neighborhood we pass by a dozen hookers hustling by an adjacent row of hotels. From Forty Sixth to Fiftieth streets, from the Doral to the Marriott, past the Waldorf and to the Loews, business is booming for these hotel-bound streetwalkers.

The women flirt with any guy that comes by. It doesn't matter if it he's young or elderly, pedestrian or driver. The women make their presence known. But when they see Tim and I walking in their direction, most scatter. Others glare at us with suspicion. Obviously our conservative sport coats and standard gray dress-pants, combined with our size (Tim is about 6'4, 260, while I'm 6'0, 225), gives us the aura of police detectives. Even the beers wrapped in brown paper bags don't change that opinion.

One of the girls eventually asks who we are. A young tough-looking hooker with one hand on her hip and the other grasping a shoulder bag, comes right out and asks, "What are you guys, cops?"

"Naw, we're not cops," Tim replies.

"You sure the hell look like cops."

Tim tells her we're from Palace security, on a break. My eyes widen, signaling my disapproval. The hooker notices my reaction.

"Don't worry, I won't tell on you," she says with a wry smile.

We stand quietly for a moment, and Tim blurts out, "How much is a blow-job going for these days?"

She gives a price, maybe forty-five bucks.

"Do I get a hotel employee discount?" he asks.

The hooker and I both laugh. Tim stares at her, waiting for a reply. He's serious about getting a bargain hummer.

While Tim follows his line of friendly questioning, I take a close look at the thirtyish prostitute. She isn't a bad looking woman. A tad bit sleazy for my taste, but hardly unattractive. I wonder what had led a decent-looking girl like this to a life of hustling.

I slip into my own little world for a moment, puzzled with the possibilities. Then she throws me off course when she asks "Well, what about you?"

"Huh?"

"Are you looking to have some fun also?"

I look at Tim, then back to her. With a touch of confused annoyance in my voice, I abruptly ask, "How the hell did you end up out here?"

It becomes quiet. Neither Tim nor his new friend know where I'm going with this.

"Don't get me wrong," I continue, "I'm not trying to bust your chops, but please tell me, how the hell did you get into this business?"

Without hesitation she replies, "My mother was a Madame. My aunt was a hooker."

She says this without a hint of shame, like a third grader who gets up in front of the class and declares, "My Mommy is a nurse and my Daddy is a fireman."

I need to find out more about this strange woman, about her bizarre life, just out of curiosity.

"Aren't you worried about getting killed by some psycho?"

"I don't worry about it."

She pauses for a moment, seemingly deep in thought.

"Uhh, look at it this way. You could get killed walking across the street, right? Well, it doesn't mean that you give up walking, does it? That's the chance you take."

Tim and I look at each other, amazed at her distorted reasoning.

"You must take some precautions, don't you?"

"Oh, sure." Counting on her fingers, as if keeping track of each brilliant point she made, she says, "First of all, I don't get into anyone's car. If they have a car, I tell them to park it and then we take a cab. Second, before I go to an apartment or a hotel, I call my pimp and let him know where I'm going."

"What happens when you meet somebody you like? How can you possibly get a boyfriend when you're a hooker?"

"My pimp is my boyfriend," she says with an unabashed grin.

It gets quiet. Neither Tim nor I have anything to say in response. Uncomfortable from the silence, she begins to justify her entry into the world of prostitution.

"Listen, I've got a house in Jersey, two brand-new cars and about a hundred and forty thousand dollars stashed away."

She pauses again, as if struggling to convince herself of the truth in her next declaration.

"I'm very happy."

Maybe she does own a house, a nice car, had a comfy bank account. But she doesn't seem convinced of her statement of happiness.

She asks us to leave, reminding us that we look like cops.

"You're scaring away potential customers," she says.

"Maybe I'll come visit you sometime," Tim tells her as we walk away.

She cracks a squinty-eyed grin before walking in the opposite direction.

"You're not really gonna pay her a visit, are you?" I ask.

Tim just smiles.

The following night, in the middle of my compulsory three-hour nap (what other professions would call a break), the phone rings, waking me. Must be time to go back on patrol, I'm thinking. Picking up the phone, assuming it's the other officer's turn to rest, I mumble, "I'll be down in few minutes.

"You'll be up in a few minutes if you want to," the voice on the other end of the line says excitedly.

I emerge from a deep sleep. Dreamland, in fact. I pause for a moment, wondering if I'm still dreaming.

"Steve, wake up! It's Tim." He chuckles and says, "I'm in room 1018 with Felicia." *Room 1018, room 1018, room 1018*, I whisper to myself. *Why does that sound familiar?* Ahh, how could I forget? I'm in room 1019, right next door. Two questions remain, however.

"Who the hell is Felicia? And why did you wake me up already? It's only three o'clock. I only got two hours sleep, man. I've got another hour to go."

"Felicia is the hooker we were talking to last night on Lexington. The answer to your second question is, you've got to see her tits! They are huge! I just nailed her. You've gotta see these titties flop. Unbelievable."

"What's unbelievable, Tim, is that you've got a prostitute in bed with you at your place of employment. Are you out of your mind?"

Ignoring my question, he says, "You'd be out of your mind if you don't let me send her over to you. She's got double D's, man! Double D's! Here, I'll put her on the phone. Maybe she can talk some sense into you."

"No, Tim, I don't want to talk to..."

A velvety smooth voice cuts me off in midsentence. It's Felicia.

"Hi handsome. You want me to come suck you off?"

"Please put Tim back on the phone."

"I'll only charge you thirty dollars. House special. Just promise that you won't bust me if you see me in the hotel again, all right?"

"I'm not promising you anything. Give the phone to Tim, now."

Tim gets back on. *The phone*, that is.

"So what are you going to do?"

"I'm going back to sleep, Tim. That's what I'm going to do."

"Okay. Your loss."

The fact that Tim brings this hooker into the hotel, when our job is to keep such people out, isn't the main reason I'm irritated. What irks me is that this ignoramus trollop now has something on us. If we ever get into a situation in the future where we need to arrest her, we'll have to look the other way.

Tim handed her a free pass. And I'm sure Felicia spread the word that you could buy Palace security.

Just like any other professionals, these ladies of the night must network with one another, in some way. And what reason would they have *not* to pass along such information? It makes their job easier and more profitable, of course. Knowledge, even for hookers, is power.

An undue amount of prostitutes flock to the hotel after Tim's meeting with Felicia. I don't know if it's a coincidence or what. Surprisingly, the number of thefts doesn't multiply with this increasing flood of hookers, however. They occur from time to time, nothing unusual about that. But what's unusual is that I no longer let it frustrate me. I'm beginning to think that Tim is right. Supply does meets the demand. And demand for service increases the supply. Also, when the guests roll the dice, it's solely their problem if the bets turn out to be unworthy of the risk.

He'd Kill Me If He Found Out

The guys from the four-to-twelve shift one night advise us that a group of men renting two bordering rooms have been holding a whore-a-thon for several hours. At least a dozen call girls separately arrive over time. We expect this to continue for at least a little while longer.

Almost as soon as we began patrolling the lobby we come across a couple of girls going to rooms 1725 and 1726. Most of them return less than five minutes later, shaking their heads in seeming disbelief as they exit. Hooker after dejected-looking hooker goes upstairs and comes right back down. This continues for hours.

The traffic on the way to these rooms eases after one particular hooker arrives. Rather than splitting after a few minutes, she stays up there more than sixty minutes. This is unusual, under the circumstances.

Even more surprising is receiving a phone call from a woman identifying herself as the "agency" manager catering the ABC-TV executives' party.

"I am quite concerned for the safety of one of my girls," she says. "It is indeed possible that she is being held against her will."

"So what the hell do you want me to do about it?" I say with a laugh.

"Well, if you do not assist me in determining the status of this girl, then I am afraid that I will have to call the authorities."

The way she spoke to me, you'd think she had sent a rental clown, a magician or a pony, rather than dozens of prostitutes, to entertain these seemingly insatiable guests. In her eyes, I guess she *was* simply supplying the entertainment or delivering a multi-course meal. I wouldn't have cared, but she put me on the spot. In typical New York fashion, I barked back.

"Then call the cops if you feel so compelled to do so," I respond, mimicking her pseudo sophistication. "Do you really think I give a damn? Go ahead. Call 9-1-1. I'll wait at the door for the cops."

She pauses, then apologizes for her tone.

"I'm just concerned for her safety," she explains. "I've been told that these men are a bit strange, and now no one's answering the phone in their room."

Now she takes on a dignified tone. Although she knows she's wrong about copping an attitude with me, she seems truly concerned for the missing-in-action hooker. She begins to backpedal, furiously

"Please, is there any way you can assist me? I don't want any problems."

"All right, I'll tell what I'm going to do," I reluctantly tell her. "I'll walk past the room, see if she's screaming for help or something. If she is, then of course I'll call the cops myself. If not, then it's up to you to decide what the next step is going to be. Either way, I'm not knocking on the door. Call me back in 10 minutes."

I rise to the seventeenth floor and tiptoe past the rooms in question. After traversing the floor back and forth, listening intently, all that I hear is the sounds of men talking—and a woman giggling. If they're holding her against her will, then they're tickling her while they're at it.

The Madame calls me back and I tell her everything seems okay. After we hang up, the "missing" hooker leaves the hotel, replaced by a steady stream of other whores. One of them, a beautiful, Italian-American girl, also exits the party quickly, like most do throughout the night. She uses the pay phone in the lobby, then sits on the couch, looking irritated. My partner and I approach her, but not to apprehend her. Instead we seek to put to rest the unanswered question of why they keep coming down so soon—and so angrily.

"That was quick," I say as I sneak up on her, trying to catch her off guard and elicit a response.

Rapidly chewing a piece of gum, she asks, "Who are you guys." She sounds like actress Marisa Tomei in her award-winning role as Joe Pesci's sidekick in the movie *My Cousin Vinny*. Genuine Brooklyn accent.

"We're from house security."

She seems unsettled. Frozen in mid-chew.

"Don't worry, we're not looking to give you a hard time," I say.

She stares, squinting as if curious, while noisily chomping away. We likewise return a glance or two, gazing upon this beautiful, yet sleazy, call girl. She's wearing a skintight, black-leather miniskirt and a stylishly tattered, dually layered blouse. Typical 80s disco gear, in other words. She lacks the curves that you might otherwise think are a precondition in the sex trade, but her inviting face and pleasant manner make up for it.

"What's the story with those jokers upstairs?" I ask. "Half of the girls that went up, came right back down."

She thinks about it, her nose crinkling as if sprayed by a skunk, then tells us how the guys verbally abused her as soon as she walked in the door.

"They were disgusting," she adds. "You wouldn't believe the things they were asking me to do. Or should I say, the things they wanted to do *to* me."

"Like what?" Phil asks.

"I don't want to repeat it, it's so disgusting."

"Come on, you can tell us."

She thinks about it for a second, unsure if she wants to reveal secrets to a couple of strangers. Soon after, she explains, "One of them wanted to screw me while at the same the other one would stuck it in my, you know..."

I finish the sentence for her.

"In your ass?"

She nods her head in acknowledgment, asking, "Can you believe it?"

Phil and I laugh simultaneously. It's easy to believe. The only thing that surprises us is her rejection of the offer. I'm under the illusion that hookers do anything for money. Even *that*.

After expressing surprise she says, "I may be a *hooker*, but I'm not a *freak*. I only do this part-time, ya' know what I mean?"

"What do you do with the rest of your time?"

"I'm a waitress. I work at a diner in Canarsie."

"You must make a lot of money as a call girl. Why waste your time waiting tables?"

"Because if I didn't have a real job, my boyfriend would wonder where I got the money."

Once again, Phil and I look at each other in disbelief.

"You have a boyfriend?"

"Actually, he's my fiance."

This is getting good. Well, at least *interesting*.

"And he doesn't know you're a hooker?"

"Are you kiddin'? He'd kill me if he found out."

I reinforced her fear.

"I'd kill you too, if you were my fiance. How the hell could you possibly hide it from him?"

"He's clueless," she says with a giggle. "He thinks I'm at nightclub with my sister."

"What if he bumps into your sister on a night you're supposedly out with her?"

"It'll never happen."

"What makes you so sure?"

"Because we work for the same agency."

"She's a hooker too?"

She responds, "Wow. You're pretty swift."

She then goes on to tell us how her sister turned her on to hooking.

"I couldn't believe how much money she was making, so I figured I'd give it a try."

She eyes me up and down.

"You're a big guy. I bet I could get you a job at my agency."

"I don't think I'd make a good prostitute," I reply, unsure of what she's getting at. She laughs hysterically. Nearly spit her gum out on the floor.

After calming down she says "No, silly. I meant that you'd make a good bodyguard, not an escort. You'd make about two hundred bucks a night. I could help you get in, if you want."

This catches my attention. The hotel is paying me well, considering we sleep half the time, but the prospect of making a couple of thousand extra dollars a month, tax-free, is enticing. The offer comes at a point in my life where I'm starting to wonder if I'm a sucker for trying to make an "honest" living. It's out of character for me to consider such an offer, but the temptation is enormous.

Somehow I come to my senses. Accepting her proposal is insanity. Besides, it's common knowledge that prostitutes, especially high-priced call girls, are controlled by organized crime syndicates, whether it be the Mafia, or Asian or Latin American gangs. I imagine that it's much easier to join than to leave.

What reminded me of this was the cardboard television box found on Park Avenue less than a week previous. A maintenance man tried to move the box, but accidentally dropped it. The dismembered limbs of an unidentified woman, who had been murdered then wrapped in sheets from a West Side hotel, spilled onto the sidewalk. I had no idea why she had been killed, nor am I suggesting the victim was a prostitute. But this horrific crime reinforced the image I already had of the people who ran these agencies. No way was I going to involve myself with them.

After thanking the hooker-waitress for the job offer, her driver arrives to pick her up. Before she leaves I ask if her fiancé thinks it's strange that she supposedly goes to a nightclub, yet comes home without smelling like liquor and cigarette smoke.

"That's easy," she says. "I just wham down a bottle of brandy before I get home. I'll be so messed up, he won't even think about it."

"Aren't you worried about developing a drinking problem?"

"Nah, I'm not worried about it."

A Lincoln Town Car is waiting. She gets in and waves good-bye as they disappear across Fiftieth Street.

Although some women probably hustle out of sheer survival, or their so-called loved ones bring them into the family business, conversations with call girls like her and hustlers like Felicia make me aware of a central motivating factor in becoming a prostitute.

Greed.

He Got What He Deserves

Despite the volume of prostitutes that come into the hotel daily, the Helmsley Palace security director never implements a written policy to address the issue. He refuses to establish procedures, believing written guidelines will create a paper trail in the event a house officer wrongfully detains a legitimate guest. One might think the "higher ups" in management would make sure there's a policy on prostitution. But since the director frequently reprimands the security staff in front of his executive-level colleagues, they more than likely assume one already exists.

No guests, not even VIPs, could bring "one of those thieving whores" into the hotel, the boss says. However insincere his rant about hookers is, he's unwavering in zeal.

Well, with one exception.

The assistant director relays a message to me from the security chief at the start of another midnight shift. "There's a group of wealthy Saudi Arabians staying in rooms 4312 and 4314, and the director wants you to avoid any confrontations with the hookers that have been going up there all night," he says.

He explains that during the previous shift, at least a half-dozen call-girls had gone upstairs to the Saudis over a few hours. More girls are on their way, he says. Just leave them be.

The hypocrisy of the instructions, in light of their otherwise crusade-like approach to hookers any other day, needs to be addressed.

"Why should they get preferential treatment?" I ask. "We try to make it difficult for everyone else. Why is it different for these guys?"

"Don't go starting any damn trouble, Peacock. Just do what the boss says and don't make waves, all right?"

"Fine. Whatever you say."

I decide to comply with their wishes—permanently. If the oil barons aren't to be disturbed, then I won't bother them or any other guests. They can bang as many call girls as they want. They apparently get turned-on by the risk involved when dealing with such women.

I'll fill out the incident report when the knockout drops wear off.

I continue to keep track of the hookers, but make little effort to keep them out. I make occasional log entries of my observations, but only to provide an illusion of security for management.

Succumbing to the forces of apathy once was non-negotiable. But apathy becomes my new partner, helping to shield me from the futility of my job and the wrath of my unpredictable boss.

This state of indifference, combined with the hypocrisy of those whom I later learned patronized prostitutes, ultimately transformed my disillusionment into amusement.

"Security! Call the guest in room 2714 immediately!" bellowed the service operator's voice from my portable radio.

I grabbed the nearest lobby phone. The guest answered by the first ring.

"This is house security. Is there a problem?"

Stuttering from anxiety, almost unable to get the words out, the guest responds, "Two woman should be coming off the elevator any second now! Stop them!"

"Why, what did they do?"

"They stole my money! Do you see them?"

I look around the lobby. Two women are walking out the door.

"Are they wearing fur coats?" I ask.

"Yes! That's them!"

I rush after the pair, but they get in a cab and drive away before I reach the door. With license plate number in hand, I run back to the phone.

"I missed them, but I got the plate number. I'm going to call 9-1-1. I'll call you right back."

"No! Don't you dare!"

"Sir, you just got robbed," I say. "I'm calling the police."

He fumbles for words, begs me not to make the call. I interrupt him, saying, "Please listen to me, sir. If my boss finds out that I didn't call the cops, I'm fired."

"No, you don't understand. This *cannot* be documented."

"Why? Do you know these women?"

Hesitantly, he reveals that he and his friend picked them up near the Waldorf. I knew what *that* meant.

"Oh, they were hookers." I exclaim. "How much did they take from you?"

"About five-hundred bucks," he sheepishly admits.

It's obvious he's withholding a key element of why he doesn't want to pursue the matter. I continue to push for answers

"I still don't understand why you don't want the police involved."

"All right, all right. I'll be straight with you. I just attended a banquet at the Waldorf. The governor was there, the mayor was there…"

"What are you trying to say?" I interject, cutting him off. "I thought you were going to be straight with me?"

He pauses before telling me the rank of his position, where he's from, who he works for. My jaw drops open, eyes widening.

He's arguably the highest ranking law enforcement official of Pennsylvania.

"I guess I should know better, huh?" he says.

"I guess you should!" I respond, tone of voice rising with each word uttered. He's vulnerable, and deserves to be hit in a sore spot with a boulder-size sarcastic comment. He gets quiet, but eventually asks, "So you're not going to call the police?"

"Nah, I'm not gonna call."

"I'd appreciate it."

We hang up and, as requested, I leave the cops out of it. But I go directly to the office to call the assistant security director at home. After explaining to him what took place, he says, "Don't call the cops, but make sure you write up an incident report."

He then asks, "Did they have drinks with the girls?"

"Yeah, I think so."

"Okay. Get a copy of the room service bill and put it in with the file. We've got to cover our ass just in case the girls put knockout drops in their drinks. I'll have the boss call you in the morning."

Before writing up the incident report I check with the front-office manager to see if this guy is really who he claims to be.

The listing next to his room number on the computer printout indicates he's telling the truth. In block letters, the line item reads: *Commonwealth of Pennsylvania.*

The next morning I get a call from my boss. At first I suspect he'll suggest that nothing happened, so I can help him protect one of his fellow law officers. Instead, he says, "Screw him. He got what he deserves. If we don't file a police report, he'll turn around and falsely accuse one of the maids of stealing his money."

One of the guys on the day shift reports the incident to NYPD. Although it undoubtedly didn't register high on the radar screen of the busy Mid-Town North precinct, which likely filed away the case soon after with no follow-up report, this incriminating file lies dormant somewhere in the city archives.

Until now it has remained unknown to this true story's main character, a leader once perched upon, and perhaps still occupying, the highest echelon of Pennsylvania's law enforcement community.

After years of dealing with hookers and the men who command their attention, it's hard not to pass judgment on them. One might argue, as my colleague Tim had done, that prostitutes respond to market forces; patrons simply are given satisfaction, however bizarre or immoral that activity may be labeled by others.

Personally, I think it's a waste of taxpayer money to chase after prostitutes. But since this profession *isn't* legal, and is unlikely *ever* to become legal, danger always will sleep side-by-side with those who participate in and support this ancient trade. Consequently, my advice to anyone that gets involved in prostitution, no matter if they intend to become a hooker or just patronize one, is this: don't say I didn't warn you.

People that become hookers often plan on taking home an above-average income with minimal difficulty. What they don't anticipate is that, frequently, they don't return home at all.

Out-of-town johns who feel it's okay to get a quickie from a hooker after a business meeting also should be forewarned. Instead of bringing home postcards of the Empire State Building and miniature figurines of the Statue of Liberty as evidence of your travels, you might find that the only thing you're bringing home is an empty wallet for your kids and a communicable disease for your wife.

PART V
Street Survivors

Get Outta Here, Ya' Bum

A homeless man, tight-jawed and sneering, stands outside the Fifty-First Street entrance, several feet from the hotel's revolving doors. With each exhale he presses his lips together, as if trying to regulate a pressured burst of air that's emerging internally. Nostrils flare, then retract. Eyes bulge. He clenches his fists at his side, arms stiff and pointing downward like crutches. Shredded strips of grayish-brown cloth sewn together resemble a shirt and pants. Icicles line the rim of the Palace veranda above his head yet he lacks a jacket.

Though his body language and facial expressions are visible to me, street sounds that otherwise would go with my view of this bitter man are muted by a series of brass-framed glass panels at the entrance. Muffled laughter and the tapping of piano keys seep through the cracks of the closed doors of Harry's Bar. What I hear *inside* swims around the opposing image of the vagrant *outside*.

Every few moments a pair of guests exits the bar, spilling an abruptly amplified volume of chatter and music into the space separating me from him. This contrast of image and sound is about as mismatched as having the soundtrack to *Mary Poppins* piped into a theater featuring *Schindler's List*.

He makes no attempt to enter the lobby. Fixated on one spot, the stranger stares contemptuously inside.

Mario, the new security supervisor, approaches and asks why I hadn't told the man to leave.

"He'll be gone soon. Besides, he's not on hotel property."

"Well I don't want him there," he tells me. "Let's get rid of him."

He calls for back-up. Another house officer joins us, as does Sanchez, one of the night cleaners, who happens to know karate.

The vagrant's teeth pinch the inside of his top lip, eyes squinting as if trying to fire imaginary lasers—as the four of us walk toward him at a quickened pace. But instead of looking concerned for his personal well-being as we approach, he hurls a silent cloud of anger in our direction, catapulted by the expression on his face.

Our fearless leader, obviously trying to impress his new crew, steps outside first, belittling the vagrant and unnecessarily heightening the situation's intensity. Mario is a forty-something Bronx Italian-American, a potbellied and matchstick-legged figure who appears to be swallowed whole by an ill-tailored double-breasted suit. Nonetheless, he advances on our subject like he's *The Incredible Hulk*.

"Get outta here, ya bum, before I kick your ass," he shouts.

Without hesitation the stranger plants a roundhouse punch on Mario's face, splitting his lip. Mario raises his hand to his mouth, sees a streak of blood that's painting his pointer finger. Rag Man steps back ready to *throw down*, notwithstanding the number of opponents.

Mario deserves to get popped, and not just for being an arrogant show-off. He fails to assess the situation before opening his mouth, ignoring the possibility of a violent response. Let's face it, folks, only a fool thinks a destitute black man living on the street would—or *should*—tolerate such nonsense from a belligerent white guy coming out of a luxury hotel draped in a suit.

Despite Mario's miscalculation, he's been assaulted. We have to back him up. His attacker must be knocked down.

Everyone present gets in a few punches, just to make sure the perpetrator is neutralized. Unfortunately, Mario's assailant emerges from the dust of the sidewalk, refuses to run. Worse, he puts his fists in the air, prepares to brawl. For a second time, the man is quickly subdued, but not before Mario introduces his size-twelve wingtips to the guy's ribs, repeatedly.

"Alright, Mario, cut it out before you kill him," I say.

"Look what he did to my lip!" Mario responds, wiping more blood, which now reaches his chin. He lets loose a torrent of profanities before kicking the downed man one more time.

Moaning, writhing on the ground, he holds both sides of his torso. Wobbling, it takes him a few seconds to get back on his feet. He staggers across the street, and we return to the lobby.

A few minutes later I go back outside to see if he's all right, or at least not vomiting blood because of a punctured organ. He's leaning against a car, still holding his arms to his ribs, which I can only assume are severely bruised if not fractured .

Ten minutes later, he's back at the revolving door, unsteady on his feet but remaining upright.

"I can't believe this stupid…," Mario says, trailing off as he heads toward the exit.

"Wait a minute, Mario, wait a minute. You're all excited. Let me talk to him instead," I say.

"Talk to him? Waddaya mean 'talk to him'? I should give him another beating, never mind talk to him!"

"I'll take care of him, Mario, just relax."

I open the exit door, a few inches at a time, signaling to the haggard man that our conflict is over.

"Yeah, you all think you're better than me," he responds. "Talkin' to me like I'm a dog."

Getting pummeled wasn't mentioned. Only Mario's condescension concerned him, it seemed.

"Well I'm gonna tell you like it is, man to man," I say. "That guy shouldn't have talked to you like that, I know. But you can't be hanging around this entrance and not expect someone to say something to you. Why don't you just leave and save yourself the trouble."

He stares without speaking, awkwardly shifting his feet every few seconds as he loses balance.

"Do you need a doctor?" I ask.

"I don't need nothin' from you," he says before stumbling away. "You hear? Nothin'."

Choir Boys

Christmas time. The expanse of the Palace lobby is adorned with rows of poinsettias and towering floral arrangements laced with handcrafted angels. Round, red-ribboned wreaths wider than the tires of earth-moving industrial trucks hang from the top of three cathedral-length windows at the mid-point of the center stairs. The image of St. Patrick's Cathedral, perched across the street on Madison Avenue, fills every pane of glass.

The Harlem Boys Choir stands perched on the stairs in the middle of this holiday spectacle, spread across several rows at varying intervals of carpeted steps. Its melodies sail through the lobby, halting the most rushed guests who pouring from the hotel elevators.

The event draws in passers-by from the street—including a deranged, albeit passive, street lady, foaming at the mouth.

She slices a path through the crowd with little effort. Some people in the audience are fixated on the choir, unconcerned with what appears to be another pushy New Yorker making her way to the front row. Others exit the scene, fleeing the stench of rot and accumulated sweat emanating from the disturbed woman's skin and oil-streaked clothes.

She makes no threatening moves, neither toward the group of African-American boys or the predominately White observers. On the contrary, this street person—whose eyes reveal scrambled thoughts and the processing of distorted images—sways gently from side to side in cadence with the tune. An angular smile breaks her otherwise static expression, spilling more saliva onto her dry, cracked lips. Her vocal cords release a staccato series of high-pitched groans of relief. Her head tilts back, smile widening, like a baby looking upward to Mommy from the confines of a crib.

Her abject appearance and spoiled chicken-soup odor startles the audience, regardless of the joy she exudes. Having seen this woman on an increasingly frequent basis in recent months, fearful that her fragile state of mind may snap from one day—or moment—to the next, I grab her by the wrists, gently twisting her arms behind her back in order to escort her out the door. She fades into the rush and flow of Midtown pedestrians.

I return to the choir performance. Stone-faced stares cause me discomfort, and I return the gaze with a shrug of the shoulders, as if silently communicating, "It was for your safety, people." My bouncer-like reaction is for the benefit of all present, a response to a potential hazard, but it isn't universally received.

I begin to second-guess my actions. Before allowing myself to consider whether I deprived a suffering human being from finding relief—for the first time in years, for all I knew—from the crushing oppression of inner demons, I quash the chance of entertaining that possibility. Up goes the emotional wall. Self-preservation over self-realization.

Bozo, We're Exercising

Effectively dealing with street people in and around the Palace requires a balancing of emotions. Getting the job done—namely, the tasks of keeping them out or ejecting them quietly when they get in—requires compassion, but not naivete, aggressiveness, but without being abusive or condescending.

This doesn't mean that force never should be used. It's just that, at least in my experience, it's got to be a means of last resort. Having a Neanderthal mentality when approaching a homeless trespasser only increases the odds of unnecessary conflict and bothersome litigation.

It's wise to proceed with what I call *contained assertiveness*, since many street people have nothing to lose. If you promise to have them arrested, you end up with provocation instead of discouragement. I mean, what can the police do? Lock them up? So what. Threatening your subject with the prospect of three free meals and a roof over his or her head for the day—in street parlance, 'three hots and a cot'—even if it *is* in a jail cell, isn't much of a deterrent.

Mr. McDougall is a homeless man who holds a low-paying, part-time job and lives in a shelter Monday through Friday. On the weekend, when the shelter is dangerous and overcrowded, he usually picks a hotel and sneaks into a vacant room.

Despite having been arrested for trespassing at the Palace several times, he continues to return, rarely with difficulty, and, more often than not, without being detected. Since he can wash at the shelter and has the resources to buy clothing, he's hardly discernable from actual hotel guests, thereby enabling him to blend in with the crowd and enter an elevator without being challenged.

I couldn't blame McDougall for trying to live—or at least sleep—comfortably every once in a while at the expense of my employer. Upon considering the vast sums of money intentionally squandered within this building while people clothed in rags slept along it's perimeter on the sidewalk, his expression of contempt for the rich and powerful is somewhat understandable.

In other instances, however, my empathy level for such people bottoms out.

My shoes screech to a halt on the polished Italian marble of the mezzanine bathroom. As I step inside, I look to my right, stopping in my tracks at the sight before me.

A vagrant has his pants unzipped and pulled down to his ankles as he leans over the sink. He's got his private parts draped over the edge of the wash basin.

The aroma of unwashed butt permeates the room. For a second I think I'm imagining things. I look away, then back again. He's lathering his penis, reaching to and fro the dispenser for more soap, scrubbing furiously and lightly laughing as he does so. But then he stops, bites his bottom lip and realizing he has an audience, snaps his head and neck to the left. I want to walk away, but his dead-serious stare and haunting laugh throws me off-balance, as if freezing my steps. This expression on his face, combined with accumulation of dry, whitened saliva at the corners of his mouth, is enough to make the bravest man fear for his safety. His sudden switch in demeanor screams out 'sociopath.'

As quickly as he stops washing and starts giggling, he returns to his main chore of washing his crotch. More soap, a little more hot water, rinse the hands. Start the process over.

"What the hell are you doing?" I blurt out. Bright question, I realize.

He pauses again, then looks at the ceiling. Without turning toward me, he refocuses his gaze on the mirror before him, breaking into a wheezing fit of laughter, staring at his reflection as he does so. Between that sick laugh, the well-worn Army infantry jacket he's wearing, and the fact that he's scrubbing his nuts in public, it's impossible not to view him as a potential threat to myself and any unfortunate guests that might unknowingly approach him. I have to get him out of the hotel, quickly

"Put your dick in your pants and get the hell out of here," I order him.

He continues with his primary task as if I'm not there. Nothing registers. This guy's seriously ill upstairs. The situation just isn't worth fighting over.

No one else is around, so I settle for standing outside the door to steer people away. It's easier than arguing, or even worse, wrestling with Stinky.

The first person that tries entering the bathroom doesn't heed my warning.

"Excuse me, sir, I'm with house security. The men's room is temporarily…" He dismisses me with the wave of a hand and goes in anyhow.

But no sooner than the door clicks behind him, he does an about-face. He raises a hand to the side of his head, cupped at his left eyebrow, as if preventing any chance of making eye contact with me. He knows his initial reaction was unwarranted. There's no hiding it. He scurries out the Madison Avenue exit.

Mr. Clean leaves soon after.

On another occasion I'm summoned to the adjacent ladies room, where someone reportedly is laying on the floor. No further info is available, so I waste no time responding. I sprint up the staircase, guessing that someone has dropped dead from a possible heart attack or seizure.

Instead, I find two women, both in their late thirties or early forties, fully-clothed for winter, doing stretching exercises on the ground like a couple of Olympic hurdlers. The smell of body odor wafts through the room—the kind of aroma that develops only when a human being is subjected to living in a box under a bridge and can't bathe for months at a time.

Just like in the last bathroom incident, I absently ask the pair of misplaced street athletes, "What are you doing?" They look at each other, puzzled. Then, like a couple of flamingos, they respectively shake their heads, purse their lips and return their gaze toward me.

The one on the right responds, "What the hell does it look like we're doing, bozo. We're exercising!"

I look at the pathetic site on the floor, in disbelief at what I just heard. Bozo?

"Get up and get out," I say.

The woman to my left, slightly younger than her partner, timidly—and sincerely—asks, "But where are we supposed to exercise then?"

"Are you guests here at the hotel?"

"No, but…"

"Well, this isn't a Jack LaLanne health spa, ladies. We don't even let paid guests exercise on the floor. Now get out."

In a strictly business sense, it's reasonable (and lawful) to eject trespassers, particularly when they pose a threat to the well being and/or hygiene of hotel occupants. When someone pays to stay at a place like the Palace—or a downtown Holiday Inn, for that matter—they don't want to worry about being harassed by the demented or sitting on an unusually ripe and soiled toilet seat in the ladies lounge.

It wasn't easy, but I had to accept the cold reality of the situation: Security was provided to protect the guests, not to dispense social services. I kept my job so long as their patronage continued. The less that guests saw "undesirables" (a category I'm sure that even the employees fell under, in the eyes of some), the more likely they were to come back.

Accepting these economic realities didn't make it easier to escort people to the gutter. As each year went on, I dealt with an expanding number of lost souls. My resistance to the nighttime influx of the homeless was wearing down. I found it increasingly difficult to view my job from a purely capitalist perspective.

I'm Gonna Live Forever

While struggling to remain awake, seated on the lobby couch, I see a woman wearing an ear-to-ear grin entering the hotel from Fifty-First Street. It's 2:30 a.m. I'm not feeling ambitious. Remaining seated, I hope she's just passing through. Besides, she looks crazed and not worth dealing with if it can be avoided. There are no guests around. I decide it's easier to let her enter one door and exit through the other without a confrontation.

Instead of continuing her rapid pace, she yanks her shirt off and runs into Harry's Bar. By the time I sprint across the lobby she has already taken off her pants and jumped from a chair to a tabletop, dancing wildly—arms swinging, legs kicking—in front of a group of male housekeepers. Despite her shriveled breasts and emaciated, crack-addicted body, the cleaners love every minute of it, clapping and whistling while cheering in Spanish.

She's a pathetic sight, but it's a somewhat welcome diversion for a bored midnight crew on break.

Much to the dismay of the audience, the entertainment has to be terminated. As usual, the standard, "What are you doing?" is uttered in vain.

She takes a deep breath, before shouting, "It's Labor Day, and ahhhm celebrating!"

Three weeks had passed since Labor Day. She must have been doing some serious celebrating.

Bizarre, bordering on comical, her comment is in some way a scream for help, whether she knows it or not. She's a lost individual, wandering aimlessly through the streets of Manhattan, undoubtedly addicted to drugs. In a different context, I also feel lost, because my required course of action is to send her back to the street.

"Put your clothes on," I tell her. "It's time for you to go."

Without hesitation, she complies. But after escorting her to the sidewalk, she stops me and says, said, "You know, I'm supposed to meet someone here tonight."

"And who may that be?" I reluctantly ask.

"Michael Ray Richardson," she says, chin raised, hands on hips. "He the star of the movie 'Fame.'"

Dancing her way toward Madison Avenue, she begins belting out the film's theme song. *I'm gonna live forever*, the number proclaims.

Although never abusive towards the homeless, my treatment of them hardly qualifies me for a Nobel Peace Prize. Most of the time I intercept them at the door, having developed a psychological barrier against their pleading to lessen guilt. Other times, especially when dealing with the mentally ill homeless, it's difficult to restrain myself from laughing in a nervous reaction to their illogical responses and rambling tirades. My response had nothing to do with seeing their situation in a humorous vein.

For instance, while standing outside the hotel's Fiftieth Street entrance during a high-traffic day shift, a mentally disturbed homeless man, feet shuffling through a crowd of hundreds of people, suddenly stops and asks, "Is Gregory Peck staying here?" I point down the block and tell him, "No, he's staying at the Waldorf." I routinely pull this maneuver when seeking to send someone away. After all, what's the point of arguing?

Over the years we probably relayed dozens of street people over to the Waldorf, whose staff as far as we knew remained clueless to this technique. Then again, its workers may have quietly transferred an equal number of homeless to our location, either as a payback or perhaps because we shared the duty of deflecting the masses of vagrants sweeping through Manhattan.

Turning my attention back to the Gregory Peck fan, he faces me and asks, seriously, I might add, "Isn't there a famous English racehorse staying at this hotel?"

No, I didn't misunderstand him. He did not say "racer," as if alluding to a jockey. He meant what he said, and waited to find out whether a racehorse was in the Palace.

Not wanting to laugh in his face, I need to send him away. *Think quickly, think quickly*, I tell myself. Just keep him moving, get him back into the flow of the pedestrian bustle.

"The famous English racehorse is staying with Mr. Peck at the Waldorf," I say.

"Oh, okay."

He trudges across Park Avenue, entering, as I suggested, the Waldorf-Astoria hotel.

Slugger

In the middle of an uneventful graveyard shift, the heat in the lobby is stifling, sleep-inducing. I step outside to cool off, wake up. After taking off my glasses and rubbing my eyes, I inhale the refreshing February air and slide the frames back on my ears and nose.

A man with a baseball bat slung over his shoulder is walking in my direction, I soon realize.

He's unthreatening, more interested in adjusting the volume of a radio in his other hand. He stops about ten feet away, says hello. *Help Me Rhonda* by the Beach Boys spills into the frosty air, briefly interrupted by the whir of a passing limousine.

Maybe six-foot two, two-hundred and forty pounds, he's not the person you want to antagonize, with or without the bat in his hands. He nods his head to the beat.

"How are you?" I respond. Not much else to say at this point.

"Not bad," he says with a lack of emotion, revealing neither sadness nor joy, responding like a coworker at the water cooler on Monday morning. "Just taking a stroll, listening to my radio."

Dressed in blue jeans and a white tee shirt, he's casual but clean. He's got no recognizable accent. I'm guessing he's from the region, maybe Jersey or Connecticut, but not from the city. Probably threw his bat and stereo into the backseat of his car, drove in to the city from the suburbs, and parked somewhere in Midtown, ready to take on the world, only if necessary. Recognizing that I'm keeping a close eye on the Louisville Slugger, he assures me—conditionally—that he's not looking for trouble.

"I carry this just in case someone tries to take my radio," he says.

"Understood," I reply.

"You're not gonna try to take my radio, are you?"

"No, you don't have to worry about that," I say, glancing at the bat once again.

"I think I'd kill someone if they touched my radio. Music keeps me calm, you know."

"It's, um, well, they say it's the spice of life."

Smiling at my affirmation of his life's pleasure, he bids me a good night and goes toward Park Avenue.

The city can make you crazy, I say to myself. There are too many humans in too small an area to live functionally. It's no wonder there are so many people wandering around babbling to themselves. Even if you don't lose your mind, you're almost guaranteed to become defensive, if not hostile.

Piano Man

While most street people try to enter the hotel to use the toilet or to escape from the cold, one guy strolls in every week or so for a different reason.

To play the piano.

Never once do I see him as he enters the building. Somehow he always slips by me. I regularly find this character in the Madison Room, an ornate dining area of the Villard House, sitting behind the piano. The marble pillar-lined Madison Room provides the right backdrop for these unscheduled graveyard-shift concerts. Keeping the original charm and atmosphere of the centuries-old mansion, the room, particularly with the lights dimmed low and a melancholy tune floating through the air, borders on spooky.

Around three in the morning I find Piano Man. A bespectacled white guy in his early sixties, wearing gray slacks and an aging off-white collared shirt, he's parked behind the grand piano, hours after the restaurant closed. He taps the keys gently. The piece he's playing echoes through the Madison Room at an audible volume, yet remains low enough so as not to invite undue attention.

As on other occasions, I enter, unknown to him, and sit on a couch in the far corner of the room. I listen for a while, without saying a word. He's on the keys about an hour and a half.

I don't have a gripe with him commandeering the room at all, or even for so long. I never find him sneaking around suspiciously. As far as I know, he isn't taking breaks from his private concert to steal silverware or rip the register open with a crowbar.

So I just let him play. It's not like he'd cranking out Beethoven's Fifth. Just somber melodies. And he always leaves before I had to ask him to do so.

Except once.

The midnight housekeeping manager is in a bad mood one night and asks me to eject piano man. The cleaning crew needs to vacuum the rug, and Billy Joel's long-lost uncle is impeding progress.

This time I startle the mystery musician when I come in. He abruptly stops in mid-key.

"Sorry to break up the fun, but the show's got to end now," I say.

His mouth opens slightly, revealing surprise that his long-standing Palace schedule is interrupted, perhaps for the first time ever.

"But I'm not bothering anybody, am I?"

I pause for a moment, wondering what to do next. True, he isn't bothering anyone. In fact, I appreciate the entertainment. It beats sitting in the lobby listening to prerecorded Jose Feliciano or Frank Sinatra all night, which plays in a never-ending often torturous loop. Besides, this guy truly can play the piano, and play it well.

"That's not the point, sir. Other business has to be taken care of," I say. "I'm sorry, but it's time to go. Place has to be cleaned."

"This is most unusual," he says, his tone rising a few octaves. "This is ridiculous."

Ridiculous? Here's a guy trespassing on hotel property, using the piano without anyone's permission, and he says it's unfair.

"You've got to be kidding me," I say. "Be thankful that I let you play in here so many times without saying anything. If that's how you feel, well then I'm afraid I'm gonna have to ask you never to come back here again. Don't step foot in this building or I'll have you locked up."

He sits as if catatonic, the only movement coming from the tears rolling down on his cheeks. The silent crying turns to sobbing by time we get to the exit door. I don't feel good about it, but it has to be done. He disappears into the darkness of 51st Street.

Hotel guests, particularly those with big bucks (and even bigger egos) understandably don't want to interact with the homeless if they could avoid doing so. Let's face it. Even if you can only afford to stay at the Red Roof Inn, you don't expect to mingle with people who look and smell like they sleep on garbage.

Offended by that observation? Well, you probably never saw human beings camped out in the cold, surrounded with bags of commercial refuse to block the chilling wind, as I had increasingly seen during five years inside and around the Palace.

Keep in mind that I began working for the Helmsleys in 1987, the zenith of the "greed" decade. Times were good for many folks. Life was going so well nationwide, especially for those in the top few tiers of earnings, that the Palace and nearly all other Manhattan hotels had no vacancies for consecutive weeks and even months at a clip. There was much money floating around, and people were willing to spend tons of it on their creature comforts. New York City catered to their every whim and desire, whether for legitimate or illicit purposes.

The intensity of the good times began to change before year-end.

Celebrities continued to be visible. Extravagant displays of wealth continued, although less often. But it wasn't a coincidence that the October 1987 stock market crash and the recession a few years later that led to a dramatic drop in hotel occupancy—and a corresponding increase in the number of destitute men and women who roamed the streets.

I don't claim to have a scientific explanation for that phenomenon. Nor do I suggest there was a direct correlation between years of rising homelessness and decreasing consumption of luxury goods and services in the U.S. following Black Tuesday '87. Nevertheless, that's how it went, and progressively got worse, into the early nineties.

And Then Along Comes Mary

As cold and indifferent as my approach to managing trespassers may seem, I was, at times, so patient with the homeless, opting to encourage them to leave instead of forcibly ejecting them, that certain employees outside security thought I was too soft-hearted with them.

Sure, we were gentle, if you consider sending a human being out into the cold with no place to go as gentle.

A young and attractive Vietnamese girl begins coming into the hotel in the middle of the night to use the bathroom. Apart from the nearly two-foot long, fluorescent-colored statue of the Virgin Mary that protrudes from her carry bag—no exaggeration—she appears emotionally and unusually clean, considering she lives on the street.

She always arrives sometime around three or four o'clock in the morning, long after the hotel bars close and most of the guests went to sleep. She enters the lady's room for a reasonable time. Never leaves a mess. I decline to bother her, as long as no one makes an issue.

As soon as I see the girl coming into the hotel one night, I walk up to the kitchen on the second floor to pick up my meal, wrapping up a turkey club sandwich and putting it in a white paper bag. Returning to the lobby, I catch Mary's biggest fan her as she exits the washroom.

"Excuse me, are you hungry?" I ask.

Startled, she becomes defensive, assuming I'm about to throw her out.

"I am homeless," she responds, revealing a slight Asian accent, "and I have nowhere to go. Please, sir, I do not wish to cause trouble."

"It's okay, I'm not gonna yell at you or anything." I partly unwrap the sandwich and motion for her to take it. "Go ahead. It's for you."

She accepts my offer, quickly bowing while struggling to smile, all the while avoiding eye contact.

The room service chef then steps onto the mezzanine. He's been watching me along, it seems.

"Who is this woman that you are giving your meal to?" he says. "I prepared it for you, not for some bum off the street."

"Hey, lighten up, Timmy," I tell him. "She uses the bathroom occasionally and she doesn't mess with anyone. I was just…"

Eyebrows raised, he cuts me off in mid-sentence, raising his voice and saying, "You mean you have allowed her to come into the hotel? The guests might pick up bugs and disease because of her. Because of *you*."

He stares at the girl, lips pressed together as if resisting the urge to vomit. Before walking away, he turns to me and says, "I don't believe Mrs. Helmsley would appreciate this."

Although technically he has no authority over me, he's the night chef, my life-line to free food as well as keeping my personal expenses to a minimum. My stomach is in his hands. Stepping on his toes could be a gastronomical disaster.

I have empathy for the homeless girl. Still, I have to choose between her hunger and mine.

"You can keep the sandwich," I tell her within earshot of Timmy, "but you have to stay out of the hotel. Don't ever come back. I'm sorry."

She curls up her lower lip and sobs.

"Are you all right?" I ask.

No response. Just clutches herself, eyes unblinking; lights out.

After she wiped a tear from her face, she said, "I am not a bad person. I have done nothing wrong."

She walks toward the door, in full mental and physical retreat, eyes focused on the carpet.

"You haven't done anything wrong," I whisper. "Not a damn thing."

Less than four hours after the midnight shift had ended, I'm already on the phone listening to my boss ranting about a "report" of lax security at night. Chef Timmy plainly doesn't waste any time ratting on me for showing a remote sense of compassion.

"Are you out of your mind?" the boss screams into the phone, "Did you actually allow some vagrant to use the lady's room?"

He deflects my explanation that I told the girl not to return.

"I don't want to hear your excuses. When the 'higher ups' start breathing down my neck, I start breathing down yours. Understand?"

"Yeah, I understand."

"You better start apprehending some trespassers and filling out incident reports," he commands. "I don't need the damn general manager on my back."

He slams down the phone. Doesn't even say good-bye.

The number of trespassers daily trying to "visit" the Palace, combined with the security director's panicky response, gives us no choice but to crack down—or at least give the illusion of doing so.

A non-guest sneaks into the hotel and falls asleep under a table in the ballroom is apprehended, processed and released. Paperwork to show the boss.

A homeless mother and daughter, both adults, along with their Chihuahua, are found in a vacant room during a routine patrol. They, too, are processed and released, but not before receiving a summons from the police. An even better file for the boss to parade around the executive office.

It's all part of the corporate chess game, and the midnight security staffers are the pawns leading the halfhearted charge.

Then winter comes.

Dropping a Dime

Escorting a homeless person out of the hotel from spring until fall is one thing. Carrying out this task in the middle of winter is a different matter. When the wind is whipping your ears and the snow is piling up at your feet, the difficulty of encouraging someone to leave is worsened. Not only does an individual's pleas for a few more moments of warmth become more persistent, more urgent, but the ability to erect a mental wall against such pleading quickly fades. It's not as if they want to come in just to use the bathroom. At this time of the year, depending on the temperature and the windchill factor, it's a matter of life and death.

One particular elderly woman begins coming into the hotel regularly throughout the season, typically sitting in the phone booth and falling asleep within minutes. Although she's prepared for the weather, wearing a hat and gloves as well as a new overcoat, it's freezing outside. I just can't ask her to leave.

The first few times she comes in we don't hesitate to tell her that sleeping in the lobby is taboo.

"I'm just using the phone," she always replies, again falling asleep soon after.

She doesn't appear homeless, but something is causing this old woman to walk around the city at four o'clock in the morning by herself.

Allowing her to sleep, regardless of her nondisruptive presence, is an invitation for trouble from management. Still, it was impossible not to feel sorry for her. I didn't know what else to do but let her rest.

A few days later she comes into the lobby again. Like clockwork, she sits and pretends to make a call. It's late, and few people are around besides a handful of employees. No one will ever know if she spends a couple of hours in there on this night. Then again, I can't continue to let her nap here. Something has to be done with, or should I say for, this elderly woman.

The lobby manager later catches me deep in thought, asking if everything is all right. I'm reluctant to be truthful, reminding myself of the incident with the chef and the Vietnamese girl. I know, or at least think, that this manager is a more reasonable colleague.

"Just so you know, James, there's an old lady sleeping in the phone booth," I tell him. "She might be homeless, but she's clean. Doesn't smell a bit." I pause, then ask, "How can I ask her to leave? It's like ten degrees out."

He peeks in the booth, then looks at me, silently. He sticks his head in for a second look, maybe even for a sniff. He says, "She could pass for a guest. Are you sure she's not registered here?"

"I'm positive. At least that was what she told me."

Reflecting on it for a second, he clears his throat and says, "Well, um, I didn't see anything."

"You mean she can stay?"

"I didn't say that," he responds. "I simply said I didn't see anything. Got that?"

He winks, then heads toward the front desk.

"Thanks, James."

He belatedly adds, "She'll have to leave when the guests start checking out, though. Get her out by six, okay?"

"No problem."

I can let her sleep for an hour or two before anyone else sees her. The sun will rise and the streets will be warmer. Asking her to leave won't be a death sentence after all.

Maybe her husband died recently and she's having a hard time dealing with it. Perhaps her apartment has been destroyed in a fire, and as a result she's ended up on the street. After picturing my grandmother in such a situation, I know that action has to be taken.

She's seated, leaning against the wall with the receiver in hand, fast asleep.

"Excuse me, ma'am."

Now awaken, she says in a soft, uncertain voice, "Oh, I was just using the phone."

I hesitate before asking, Is there any way I can help you? Is there someone I can call for you? A relative, anybody?"

"I'm calling someone right now."

"Ma'am, you've been saying that for weeks. Maybe if I call social services you can get help."

She responds, "No, I'm fine. Really."

There's nothing I can do. Can't force a person to seek help. She seems to be in a fog, of sorts, but within the bounds of reality. Her predicament is beyond my control.

She rests until a quarter to six, then leaves on her own, never to return to the Palace.

Tawana's Injustice

The assistant security chief's voice blares from my portable radio, screaming, "All house officers report to the lobby immediately! Get down here now!"

A situation is brewing.

That's too bad, because I just settled down in a room on the 23rd floor, suit and tie off, jeans and tee shirt on. It's one of the rare occasions that I'm in the room legitimately. Instead of being there to sleep for a few hours while on the clock, it's my turn to serve as the building's designated fire safety director. It's a temporary, cushy arrangement made possible by a new law requiring someone to always be on duty for this purpose in all high-rises. Being one of the first on staff that the New York City Fire Department certified for this chore, I get to sit in a room and be paid double-time just in case the alarm goes off.

It's my sole task for the last half of the four-to-twelve shift, a welcome assignment considering I've already worked twelve hours on this day. With no other fire safety person in the hotel I'm able to kick back, watch TV and hope no one triggers the alarm system.

Under hotel policy, no other security duties apply to me. But considering that my boss sounds like he's getting stomped upon in the lobby, I forego this little perk and sprint to the elevator.

Upon reaching the ground floor I find myself in the middle of thirty black folk, ranging from infants to the elderly, holding a candlelight vigil on the grand staircase. Encircled by about a dozen children is the city's high-profile community activist and future Presidential candidate, the Reverend Al Sharpton.

It's a civil crowd, but the unexpected arrival of the Sharpton crew on this otherwise peaceful January evening adds to the event's shock value, at least from the perspective of the employees. I stop in my tracks, look around. In addition to the protestors on the stairs there's a couple of dozen more standing around, candles aglow. I'm surrounded.

All eyes shoot toward the white boy with the radio in his hand. No one moves. I'm likewise locked in place. Almost uncontrollably, I tilt my head back and laugh, shouting, "Al Sharpton. Ho-ly smoke!" His cronies aren't amused. I restrain an additional compulsion to tell the obese activist that he looks like an upside down turtle that can't get right side up.

I repeat aloud, "Al Sharpton," making eye-contact with him momentarily. With a scowl he looks away.

"Peacock, get over here!" I suddenly hear my boss holler from across the lobby.

Oops. I'm so focused and amused with Sharpton that I hadn't noticed my co-workers struggling to lock the revolving doors to the Fiftieth Street entrance. Outside on the sidewalk are a hundred more Sharpton supporters trying to enter the hotel. Though the adjacent vestibules are secured, my partners are grappling with a protester who manages to slip partially through the center entryway. We spin him through the passage, returning him to the sidewalk where he belongs. It's a necessary maneuver, but has the unintended effect of causing the crowd to rally around its "heroic" comrade, chanting, "No justice, no peace! No justice, no peace!"

I suddenly realize that I hadn't thought about why this ordeal was underway in the first place, so overwhelmed we are between the rush to lock the doors and the surprise element of this encounter. I turn to Benny, one of the other house officers still sweating from his ejection of a trespasser, and ask, "What's this about, anyway?"

He shakes his head and squints, as if pained by my as-of-yet unanswerable question, asking, "How the hell am I supposed to know?"

I walk up to one of the protesters, a stern but calm-looking middle-aged black woman standing among the demonstrators in the lobby, and say with excessive caution, "Please don't take this the wrong way, I'm just curious." I pause for a moment before asking, "What are you doing here? What's the purpose of all this?"

"In light of the fact that less than five-percent of the population controls over ninety-percent of the wealth in this country," she says, "we are proposing that those who possess such wealth, such as the Helmsleys and the Trumps, should reserve at least five-percent of their resources, or perhaps five-percent of the hotel rooms they own, for the purpose of housing the homeless."

After giving this some thought for a few seconds, I respond, "I don't agree with that proposal, but I understand where you're coming from."

On one level the plan is a much-needed call to action—a lofty but respectable attempt to address one of the city's most pressing issues. But coming back down to reality, demanding a private-sector hotel to transform a segment of its operations into a public homeless shelter in no small way stretches the bounds of reasonableness.

Just as I'm about to thank her for clarifying the situation, one of the protesters—a tall, burly man wearing an Muslim-style skull cap—points his finger in my face and shouts, "You don't understand a damn thing, because you white!"

"I strongly suggest that you get your finger out of my face."

"You white people just don't care," he responds.

The "reasonable" woman whom I had just spoken with nods in agreement. Her stated desire to become a voice for the homeless is mere hyperbole. The ensuing chant from outside verifies my suspicions.

"No justice, no peace! No justice for Tawana!" the mob repeats in unison.

All of the employees present looked at each other in disbelief.

One of the bellman, a feisty, stereotypical Brooklyn Italian, asks, "No justice for Tawana? Are these people out their minds?"

The Tawana they're speaking of is none other than Tawana Brawley, the young, African-American girl who made national headlines when she claimed to have been kidnaped, raped and smeared with human feces by a group of white men in upstate New York.

Al Sharpton and company continued to exploit Brawley's allegations as a publicity springboard, despite the findings of a grand jury that her entire story was concocted. Perpetuating the Brawley mythology for the sake of advancing Sharpton's personal agenda was despicable in itself, but drawing out the matter under the guise of speaking for the homeless sank him to a new low.

"You are an ignorant bastard," Anthony the bellman screams at the towering protester, "You don't give a damn about anybody but yourself."

No justice, no peace! No justice for Tawana!

The chanting amplifies. Protesters begin kicking and beating the doors. A glass panel cracks, and we wait for the entirety of the entrance to collapse from the pressure being exerted by the increasingly agitated crowd.

An army of blue-shirted police in riot gear enter through the opposite side of the hotel and spread out across the lobby, standing as if ready to crack some heads, but remaining silent and waiting for orders from an elderly, ruddy faced officer who enters soon after. His presence is highlighted by the white hat adorning his head, signifying he's from among the upper echelon of NYPD and reflecting the sensitive nature of contending with yet another act of traffic-stopping civil disobedience by Reverend Al. The presence of the cops is all that's needed to control the mob, which wisely declines to make waves with the baton-wielding sea of blue. The protesters on the outside cease their efforts to enter, while the majority of those in the lobby exit.

The police commander tells the assistant security chief to once again ask Sharpton and the remaining demonstrators to leave. It's a formality that's needed to seal the department's legal justification for hauling them away, since the public technically has limited access to the lobby. The boss carries out the order. Sharpton says nothing and looks away, as if annoyed by this request, and Sharpton and five others are subsequently arrested. The rest of the crowd disperses after its leader is handcuffed and taken away.

All that remains are wax drippings on the rug. A Twilight Zone surrealism envelops the air as we process the sudden, relative absence of people. As the evening progresses, many employees jokingly say, "Did that really happen?"

Sure, the event occurred, but on some level nothing really happened. The event, reported by the New York Times the next day as the Martin Luther King Jr. March for the Homeless, had begun at the Plaza Hotel on Central Park South, proceeded along Fifth Avenue to Trump Tower, then stopped by every posh establishment along the route to the Palace. It was a chance to make an effective social statement to the thousands of wealthy residents and visitors in this exclusive section of Manhattan. Instead, the marchers polluted the issue of homelessness with cries of "No justice for Tawana."

The following day the homeless and the insane continued to march onward, aimlessly, cups in hand.

0-595-30464-8

Made in the USA
Columbia, SC
14 February 2021